SIBERIAN EXILE

SIBERIAN EXILE

Blood, War, and a
Granddaughter's
Reckoning

Julija Šukys

UNIVERSITY OF NEBRASKA PRESS   *Lincoln and London*

Library of Congress Control Number: 2017946600

Set in Arno by Rachel Gould. Designed by N. Putens.

Frontispiece: Ona in Siberia, 1956. Private collection. Courtesy of the author.

For my son

The journey here was very easy . . .
but the road back is much harder.

Ona, letter from Siberia, August 25, 1957

Contents

Illustrations

MAPS

Acknowledgments

I gratefully acknowledge the Canada Council for the Arts, the Research Board of the University of Missouri System, and the Research Council of the University of Missouri, Columbia, for supporting the writing of this book.

I offer my deepest gratitude to Darius Zubrickas, who has been my ally in this project from day 1. I thank the archivists and librarians at the World Lithuanian Archives, Kent State University Archives, the Lithuanian Special Archives, Šakiai Public Library, the U.S. Holocaust Memorial Museum, and the Vincas Kudirka Museum. Heartfelt thanks go as well to the many friends, family members, colleagues, archivists, and librarians who supported my work in countless ways: Elena Razlogova, Anton Hanevich, Vasily Hanevich, Mindaugas Martišius, Svetlana Jarumbavičiūtė, Yana Pugach, John-Paul Himka, Maggie Paxson, Charles King, Saulius Sužiedėlis, Medeinė Tribinevičius, Violeta Davoliūtė, Lawrence Ries, Tauras Bublys, Andrew Leland, Joanna Hearne, Alexandra Socarides, Steve Weinberg, Colleen Mohyde, Bridget Barry, David Read, Romas Treideris, Arūnas Bubnys, Nida Gelažis, Laimonas Briedis, Izaokas Glikas, Birutė Tamoliūnienė, and the late Algimantas Zubrickas. Finally, to Sean Gurd and Sebastian Gurd, I offer my love and gratitude, always.

Chronology

1899   Anthony is born.

1905   Ona is born.

1927   Anthony and Ona marry.

1928   Ona's elder daughter is born.

1931   Ona's middle child, a daughter, is born.

1934   Ona's youngest child, her son, is born.

1934–40   Ona, Anthony, and the children live in Klaipėda.

May 1941   The family moves to Kaunas.

June 13–14, 1941   Ona is deported to Siberia.

July–September 1941   Mass shootings of Jews take place in Newtown and elsewhere in Lithuania.

July 1944   Anthony flees westward with his children.

1947   Ona's children receive her first postcard from Siberia. Anthony and his younger daughter depart for Bradford.

1948   Ona's son and her elder daughter depart for Bradford.

1953   Joseph Stalin dies.

1954   Margarita joins Ona in Brovka.

1955   Regular correspondence between Ona and her children begins.

1958   Ona and Margarita return to Soviet Lithuania.

1965   Ona arrives in Canada.

1966   Anthony arrives in Canada.

1968   Darius is born.

1972   Julija is born.

1985   Anthony dies.

1990   Ona's son (Julija's father) dies.

1996   Ona and her younger daughter (Darius's mother) die.

2007   Julija's son is born.

2010   Julija goes to Siberia.

2014   Julija goes to Newtown.

SIBERIAN EXILE

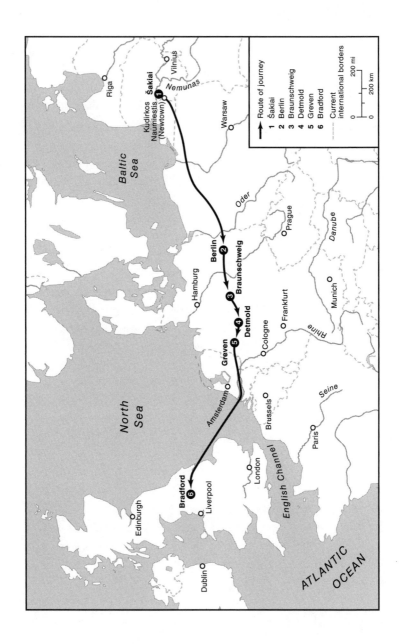

MAP 1. Anthony's journey from Šakiai to Bradford, approximately two thousand kilometers. Created by Erin Greb.

PART I

Anthony

1

Someone always pays. The question is who. And the question is how.

2

Saint Catharines, Canada, 1979.

Anthony is tall, broad, with large feet. He has huge hairy hands and shaves his head bald with an ivory-handled straight razor. On Sundays he and his wife pile into the backseat of their daughter's family car. The two aging bodies rise gently over bumps in the road and then slump to one side in unison when the sedan turns a corner.

Though he shuffles from Parkinson's disease when he walks and his hands tremble, Anthony's mind is sharp. It will never betray him. His wife's is another story. After his death six years from now, Ona will leave Saint Catharines and spend her final days in a nursing home more than a hundred kilometers away, close to her elder daughter. There, she will walk the halls, gesture to nurses and other residents, and say, "Tell them I was in Siberia."

Whenever my brother and I come to visit, Anthony teases us. He tells old-fashioned jokes we don't understand.

"How do you recognize a Russian spy?" opens one of his favorites.

"He speaks Russian?" I try. I am seven.

"No, he drinks his tea like this!" Anthony takes a cup and closes his right eye as he sips. "You see? He's removed the spoon, but he can't break the habit of closing his eye to avoid its getting poked. That's how you know he's Russian. Russians never take the spoon out."

Bewildered, I force a laugh. Truth be told, I am afraid of my grandfather. Anthony retains a hardness that served him well as a young man in the military. Even the framed photograph from his and Ona's fiftieth wedding anniversary shows him stone-faced. He proceeds to tell us children how he, a Lithuanian, used to drink tea in the Old Country—never after the (according to him) Russian fashion, with the spoon still in the cup, but through a hunk of sugar held between his teeth. He snorts, and his face softens into a rare smile.

Every family tells its children the story of who it is. Our story was of proud people forced from their homeland when the soldiers came. They took my father's mother and shipped her east of the Ural Mountains, alone. They took her by mistake. It was all a mistake, or so the story went. Her husband, Anthony, had been the target. But he had escaped, to the safety of the West, by luck and through cunning with his children.

Our job, as kids, was to learn this story and remember it. To master our grandparents' language so that, one day, we might return home from exile. The first problem in taking on this latter task was that we had never seen this home to which we were to repatriate. The second was that the story we'd been told wasn't strictly true. Important pieces of it, the complicated bits that made it hard to narrate, had fallen away.

In *The White Album,* Joan Didion writes that "we tell ourselves stories in order to live." But we also come into the world with stories—some of them distortions or even lies—tattooed on our skin. I always wanted to believe that these histories connected me to the land of my ancestors. And I have always imagined that my rightful place lay at the end of a long chain of whispering ghosts and spirits.

One of these spirits was my paternal grandmother, Ona. A deep desire to tell Ona's story has inhabited me since childhood. Even back then, I had a sense that her tale of injustice and survival was fragile and vulnerable to oblivion. And even though I knew far less about her deportation and exile than I wanted to or perhaps than I should have, I sensed that one day I would sit down and write it.

She would whisper her story to me somehow, I was sure of it. This desire to record her life grew to an urgency when I myself became a mother. I wanted to pass her story on to my son, so he too could know where he came from and who he was. So that he could take his place in the string of whispering ancestors.

But we know there are no actions without consequences, that no good intentions go unpunished. When I began reconstructing Ona's life, I imagined I was doing, for lack of a better term, a mitzvah for my family. From the wound that had shaped all of our lives so decisively—my grandmother's decades-long Siberian exile—I hoped to make something redemptive. I now see that I was naive in embarking on a project that flirted dangerously with hagiography. The universe decided to teach me a lesson by handing me a truth I neither expected nor desired. Perhaps the discovery I made about who my grandfather Anthony had really been and how my grandmother had unwittingly paid for his sins is my penance for taking a kind of pride in Ona's victimhood. Maybe it was a warning against claiming an ancestor's pain and survival as my own.

But I think my greatest sin was to believe that this journey would or, worse, *should* be easy. My mistake was to think that I had something to teach my son rather than to learn myself. Before I could begin to tell him who he was, I had to rewrite the narrative my family had given me. And before I started to dictate my child's story, I had to ask whether I had the right to do so in the first place.

Here in North America, on this land taken through massacre, disease, expulsion, and rape, we believe in fresh starts. We pretend that everyone gets a fair shake. But not in the Old Country. There, as the Book of Exodus tells us, the sins of the father shall be visited upon the son; a boy born of a sinner will pay for his forebear's transgressions. Perhaps a girl will too, but the book doesn't specify.

Those of us born in the New World tend to reject this ancient view. The Nile may have turned to blood, we say, but here our rivers run clean. They wash our grandfathers' and fathers' sins away.

Or do they?

3

I grew up not far from Toronto, on the banks of the Credit River. By Canadian standards, it's a shallow and minor tributary, whose small delta has created fertile wetlands. My most vivid memories of time spent with my father are of the long walks we used to take surrounded by bulrushes and songbirds. Rivers marked his childhood too: my father was born on the Lithuanian banks of a waterway similar in size to the Credit. The Scheschuppe River (Šešupė in his—our—first language) appears as two lines that snake along the edges of a Lithuanian border city on the map that hangs on my office wall. The town once served as a gateway from Lithuania to East Prussia (today's Russian region of Kaliningrad). Its name translates as Newtown (Naumiestis, Neustadt, Naishtot) from the various languages that are now or were once spoken there.

Every day, when I get to work, I read the family names plotted on the map: Salanski, Kaplan, Silberman. I trace its carefully rendered streets, named for landmarks like the bathhouse and synagogue. Next, I follow paths that go beyond the paper's limits to territories that ancient cartographers described as belonging to dangerous creatures. *Here be monsters,* they wrote. Out beyond the known world lay the realms of fast-running, backward-footed Abarimon and dog-headed Cynocephali. But monsters can be deceiving. The Eastern monks who painted Saint Christopher as he carried the young Christ across a river sometimes portrayed him as a giant Cynocephalus. Storybooks tell us that monsters can be humane. History books and archives remind us that humans can be monstrous. And, yes, beyond Newtown's edge once lurked the cruelest creatures of all, men with guns.

I've hung the map despite my husband's warnings. "It's in bad taste," he says. "Macabre." When colleagues pop their heads in my doorway, they instinctively grin at it above my head. It's rare to see a document so large, so detailed, and so obviously handmade. But once their eyes settle on the block letters printed at the bottom right-hand corner of the map, they understand what they're looking at:

MASS GRAVE

OF ALL WOMEN

AND CHILDREN

3RD DAY IN ELUL-5701

SEPTEMBER 16TH 1941

An arrow points to a place beyond the paper's edge.

They see this, and a shadow descends. Conversation cuts short. My colleagues excuse themselves and take their leave. Though I respect their discomfort, I leave the map on the wall, because I need this object of contemplation. For me, it serves as proof of how much I still do not know. Of how far I must go to finish what I've started.

Hand drawn in ink, the map of Newtown measures almost one square meter. It came to me via a friend many months after I first opened my family's files from the Secret Police Committee (KGB). She found the map while digging in the U.S. Holocaust Memorial Museum in Washington DC and sent me a digital copy. I had it printed onto a huge sheet of paper.

The creator of this document was a native of the city he drew. A young man in 1922, Ralph Goldberg left Newtown for Chicago and thus escaped the fate of so many. Almost fifty years later, he began to plot his childhood streets from memory.

The map pleases me because in it I recognize something I do too—that is, meticulously piecing together detail upon detail. I like

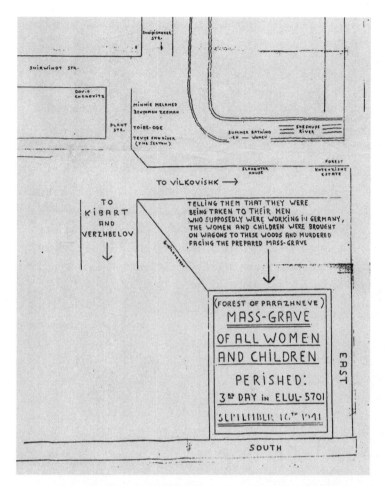

FIG. 1. Detail from the map of Newton (Naishtot) by Ralph Goldberg.
U.S. Holocaust Memorial Museum.

the way the mapmaker has sketched a plan and pondered what's
absent. But the thing I love most about this rendering of Newtown
is that it remains a work in progress. At the bottom of his map,
Goldberg has extended an invitation to collaborate:

> There is enough space for anyone to write in a missing name in his
> proper place or to correct any error.

The plan of Newtown also includes a dedication, which I read and reread:

> My intention in making this map is—perhaps in the future generations, a grandchild or a great-grandchild will, out of curiosity, unfold [it]. He may accidentally recognize a familiar name that he heard years ago in his parents' or grandparents' home. He will also read about how and when the terrible Holocaust happened. It is my hope that this will remind him not to forget and not to forgive.

The friend who sent me the map believes I'm the heir its maker had in mind.

"You are the grandchild," she writes. "He drew this thing for you."

I, however, am not so sure. Yes, I am a grandchild of Newtown. But surely I'm also the wrong one. The wrong kind. The mapmaker's last sentence, in particular, fills me with dread.

4

The words "Lithuanian Soviet Socialist Republic's Secret Police Committee (KGB)" run across the document's forest-green cover. A stamp declares its contents "Top Secret." The file was opened in 1949 and closed in 1985, the year of Anthony's death. Beside the heading "Storage Term," I read, "Forever."

There can be no doubt that the record is my grandfather's; the date and place of birth are his. I open it to find a wallet-size military portrait of Anthony mounted onto a manila-hued page and outlined in blue pencil. The pages that follow, most of them typed in Russian, lay out the basis for a criminal indictment. This document is a search file. It outlines the identity of—and the evidence against—a wanted man.

Secret agents' code names translate to "Captain," "Scout," "Clover," "Dove," and "Falcon." Each reports on what his or her surveillance has uncovered. I find a great deal of material—testimony, evidence—from my great-aunt, Anthony's sister. Agents interrogated her about his movements at the end of the war and whether he corresponded with Ona upon her 1958 return to Lithuania from Siberia.

"Ona receives many parcels from her husband which he sends from England," she told them. "He is very rich."

I've had this file for three years. When I wrote to the Special Archives of Lithuania, I did so on a lark after a conversation with a fellow writer. She had asked me if I'd ever looked at my family's

FIG. 2. Anthony's photo from the KGB search file. Lithuanian Special
Archives.

KGB files and suggested I might find materials about Ona's Siberian deportation among those documents.

At the time of that conversation, I was focused solely on telling my grandmother's story. I knew little about Anthony's life and wasn't particularly curious about him. I never dreamed how such a query would change not only the book I was writing but also the understanding of who my family was, who *I* was. I didn't know how fundamentally it would alter my relationship to the past.

Of the four hundred pages that arrived, almost a hundred were KGB documents from Anthony's search file. The question of why there should be so much material on him crossed my mind but only briefly. Strangely I didn't then ask myself what a "search file" might be, though it was a term I'd never come across before. In fact, naive as it seems to me now, I found myself looking forward to reading the documents.

5

I never knew my grandfather Anthony all that well. The youngest of his five grandchildren, I resided more than an hour away from the town he'd lived in since the mid-1960s. I saw him at family gatherings and can only remember once spending the night on the Murphy bed in the apartment he shared with my grandmother. I don't recall his ever spending the night with us at our suburban home. I have no memory of the two of us ever having been alone together.

The sole member of the family who liked guns, Anthony was an excellent shot. He never learned to drive a car, but before the war, his rifle slung over his back, he used to ride a bicycle back and forth to a shooting range in the Lithuanian countryside where he was born and raised. In Canada, he invariably won the turkeys offered up as prizes for target-shooting competitions at Lithuanian community picnics.

His was a generation whose gender and birth order determined an individual's fate. The first son might inherit the farm, the second would attend the seminary, and the third would enter the military. Only a very fortunate boy would attend university. As for daughters, generally speaking, a life of cooking, of cleaning, and perhaps of fieldwork awaited them. For their part, Anthony's parents sent some of their children to become nuns and priests, since a life in the Church offered a secure future. Anthony's destiny lay with the military. To him, war and uncertainty became more familiar than peace and stability.

So it was that in 1919, at age twenty, he answered a call for volunteers and went to fight in the nascent Lithuanian army. Today the battles Anthony fought are called the Freedom Struggles.

In 1964 Anthony published a memoir about those years. A London press established by World War II exiles published the Lithuanian text. Almost four hundred pages long, *Two Wooden and Three Iron Crosses* spans two years, from 1919 to 1921. I have a clothbound copy of it on my library shelves. The book opens with his grenade training, setting up field kitchens, and leading battalions through devastated villages. The fighting was between the "Whites" (meaning anticommunist Lithuanians who had apparently adopted the nomenclature of the Russian Revolution) and the "Reds" (Russian Bolsheviks), who, after the collapse of the Russian Empire, sought to reestablish Russian control of the Baltics through Soviet rule. Curiously, there isn't much talk in the book of the primary regional conflict of the time, the Lithuanian-Polish War of 1919–20.

Lithuania had just declared independence from the Russian Empire in 1918 a year before Anthony went to war. For the first time since the days of the Grand Duchy (1341–1795), the people of this land would stand on their own feet. And for the first time ever, their leaders would speak their language, not Polish or Russian as they had done for centuries. To Anthony, a member of the last generation of Lithuanians born under czarist rule, statehood and autonomy were ideals worth fighting for. He did so valiantly, rising through the ranks and earning a chest full of medals for his efforts. In 1920 the Soviet Union concluded peace treaties recognizing independent Lithuania, Latvia, and Estonia. By 1922 all three countries were full members of the international community.

In the early 1920s, high on national pride, Anthony returned to the place of his birth—the agricultural but traditionally wealthy Zanavykija region of Lithuania on the country's far western edge—a hero.

With his battles behind him, Anthony was ready to settle down. His military prowess had made him more marriageable than ever

FIG. 3. Anthony's medal for valor, 1919. Private collection. Courtesy of the author.

before, so he had the pick of the region's beauties. A young woman with broad cheekbones and a calm demeanor caught his eye at a village wedding. Though others had courted Ona, it was the young army veteran who won her over. In 1927 the couple married. The bride was twenty-two years old; the groom, twenty-eight.

The Lithuanian government had promised free land to early military volunteers. Since Anthony had been among the first to join, I imagine his service is how he acquired the forty-hectare farm he worked together with his young wife. In contrast to so many generations before them, Ona and Anthony worked the land not as serfs but as masters.

The late nineteenth and early twentieth centuries were times of emigration and political unrest in Lithuania. Until 1924 when the U.S. Congress passed legislation severely limiting immigration from southern and eastern Europe, large numbers of young men headed for America and worked in Pennsylvania's coal mines. Others had ended up in Chicago's slaughterhouses and appeared as characters in Upton Sinclair's *The Jungle* (1906). Some of these migrants returned home after making their fortune, but many stayed and put down roots in the New World, far from the Baltic shore.

Still others studied in Austria, Germany, France, or Russia. They returned home with foreign degrees and new, often socialist ideologies that unsettled their elders. In response, conservative Lithuanian thinkers founded youth groups to combat the influence of intellectual movements like positivism and materialism. They created organizations—complete with flags, ranks, and multileveled governing bodies—to instill the values of Catholicism, family, intellectual rigor, and service. One such youth group, Ateitis, whose members are known as "The Futurists" (*Ateitininkai*), still functions today, both in Lithuania and among the North American émigré community.

Both the Left and the Right threatened Lithuania's ruling class. A 1926 coup d'état saw the country's first democratically elected president deposed and replaced by the dictator Antanas Smetona.

Smetona saw ideological enemies all around. He jailed not only leftists (among those he imprisoned was one of Lithuania's most beloved and famous writers, Kazys Boruta) and members of the extreme Right but also conservative Catholics who were attempting to play the role of intellectual counterweight, such as the Catholic thinker and university professor Pranas Dovydaitis.

As for Ona and Anthony, I know few details of their life during this period except that they had their first child, a daughter, in 1928. Their second child, also a daughter, arrived in 1931. Finally, in 1934, my father was born. No doubt, my grandparents worked hard to make ends meet, but the Great Depression of the 1930s brought a recession to Lithuania. Anthony and Ona lost their farm as a result of plummeting crop prices and a 1934 German boycott of Lithuanian agricultural products. They left my father with Ona's parents at the elders' borderland farm and moved to the city, where they tried to make a new life.

6

The years 1935 and 1936 saw mass arrests in the Union of Soviet Socialist Republics (USSR). The imprisoned and executed included Joseph Stalin's closest associates, advisers, friends, and relatives. A number of prominent Lithuanian communists counted among the victims as well. In 1937 and 1938 the Great Terror reached its height: Secret police arrested 1.7 million people all over the USSR; shot close to a million on ethnic, political, and economic grounds; and then sent more than 400,000 individuals into punishing exile in Siberia and Kazakhstan. In addition to widespread murder and oppression, a famine engineered by Stalin devastated Ukraine in 1932–33. In some cases it reduced starving people to cannibalism in a desperate attempt to survive.

Because their country managed to escape the Soviet Union's sphere of influence in the 1920s and 1930s, Lithuanians were fortunate to avoid Stalin's Great Terror. Nonetheless, despite their having front-row seats, it's unclear how many Lithuanians had either a keen interest in or accurate knowledge of events in the Soviet Union. I wonder, for example, if my grandparents had any sense of what the Bolshevik regime would bring them.

Once the Soviets annexed Lithuania, Anthony would be among those labeled "enemies of the people," a term the Bolsheviks used widely and had applied with zeal since the Russian Revolution. His name would appear on the list of those destined for Siberia.

There is no doubt that his military service alone would have sufficed for him to be slated for exile. But Anthony also had shady associations—extremist and racist affiliations that had not been part of our family lore or oral history, ones that I discovered in his KGB files instead. The revelations devastated me.

From the yellowed pages of the archival documents, I gathered that as late as 1939 Anthony had been a member of a small, underground, far-right, and radically anti-Polish, anti-Semitic organization called Iron Wolf. Founded in 1927 and comprising primarily army officers, the Lithuanian fascist group took its name from the medieval origin myth of the city of Vilnius in which a grand duke dreams of an iron wolf howling atop the hill where the city was to be founded. Though banned in 1930, Iron Wolf nevertheless continued to operate. Its members planned to overthrow the Smetona government (which itself had come to power through a coup) and even attempted to do so in 1934, the year my grandparents lost their farm and moved to the autonomous port city of Klaipėda, where Iron Wolf was especially active.

I have no documentary evidence to support my hunch, but it seems that Anthony was likely a member of Iron Wolf the year it attempted its coup. That said, his role in the organization was modest. Anthony helped distribute Iron Wolf's underground newspaper that was printed in Klaipėda.

Klaipėda (called Memel in German) had strong historic and cultural ties to Germany. Long part of the German Empire and then of the Weimar Republic, Memelland—as the region is called in German—was separated from Germany by the Treaty of Versailles in 1920. Its ties to Germany were ideological too: in February 1934, the year of Iron Wolf's attempted coup, the Lithuanian government arrested dozens of pro-Nazi Memelland activists.

Iron Wolf's leaders claimed that they accepted only "pure-blood" Lithuanians into their ranks (though how one verifies such blood purity, I don't know). The organization enjoyed support from Adolf

Hitler's Germany. Iron Wolf's primary beef with the Smetona regime, apparently, was that it was neither repressive nor fascistic enough.

Despite its radical rhetoric, it seems that Iron Wolf was responsible for mostly minor attacks, such as throwing stones at a rival party leader's car. Even so, press releases from the 1930s outline a concern that, in time, Iron Wolf would grow more violent. Archived analyses warn of heightening anti-Semitism among the organization's followers. Police reports from that era document the tracking of clandestine package deliveries, no doubt boxes that Anthony had helped fill with fascist newspapers.

Whereas the Nazis and their supporters were causing trouble in the far western regions of Lithuania, in the southeast, by contrast, the Bolsheviks—and what they could do both for and against Lithuania—were on everyone's minds.

Perhaps the Soviet annexation of Lithuania in 1940 was inevitable. Or maybe the Lithuanians, distracted and unable to resist the Soviets' offer to return their "spiritual" capital, opened the door to the enemy.

Poland had annexed the Vilnius region in 1923, causing Lithuania to sever its diplomatic relations with the neighboring country. Then, in 1939, the Red Army seized Vilnius from the Poles. Allow us a military presence on your soil, the Soviets proposed, and we'll give you your capital. The Lithuanian government agreed, though many ordinary citizens were wary of the compromise. *Vilnius mūsų, Lietuva rusų* (Vilnius may be ours, but Lithuania belongs to the Russians). This sardonic rhyme was heard in the country's cafés, streets, and farms.

In any case, causal or not, the Vilnius bargain marked the beginning of the end for Lithuania's independence. Soon the Bolsheviks not only were running Soviet military bases in Lithuania but also had taken over the entire country. With the Bolshevik regime came arrests; executions; seizures of lands, homes, and businesses; repression; terror; and deportation. What's more, the regime change destroyed already fragile Lithuanian-Jewish relations and pitted the two communities against each other.

Litvaks (Lithuanian Jews) had lived in relative peace alongside their Christian neighbors for centuries, after being first welcomed in significant numbers in 1388 and 1389 by Vytautas the Great. In twentieth-century interwar Lithuania (whose territory did not include the region of Vilnius, which was so central to Jewish intellectual life), Jews made up between 7 and 8 percent of the country's population. With schools, synagogues, prestigious yeshivas, libraries, research institutes, customs, and languages of its own, the Jewish community cultivated a separateness. But even so, there were points of contact: Jewish doctors treated Gentile patients, Jewish and Christian children often attended the same nurseries, a small number of Jewish leaders held seats as mayors and other official town posts, and numerous Jewish scholars taught at universities. From time to time, interfaith couples fell in love and married across the religious divide.

Though Lithuanian culture is full of images, stories, sayings, and jokes that poke fun at and even mock Jews, until 1941 there were no regular Polish- or Ukrainian-style pogroms. Jews felt reasonably safe in Lithuania. But with the Soviet occupation, latent animosities strengthened and surfaced. Lithuanians had the impression that their Jewish neighbors were doing well under this new communist regime and, in some cases, were even leading it. Anti-Semitism grew and spread throughout the country, fueled by nationalist propaganda that equated the Jews with the Bolsheviks.

By the time of the 1940 annexation, Anthony had moved his family out of the Klaipėda region and into Lithuania proper. They settled in Newtown, located on the country's western edge. There, he worked as a border guard at an emigration post through which Baltic Germans and Lithuanians with family or ethnic connections to Germany and Prussia could repatriate. In the spring of 1941, the emigration post closed, so Anthony returned with his family to Kaunas in May of that year and took a short-lived position as a police officer. He lost his job when local Soviet officials discovered his military past. A few months later, in the fall of 1941, Anthony would relocate to Newtown once again.

By summer solstice, Lithuania sees only a few hours of darkness. On Saint John's Eve, June 23, even small children stay up late into the night to sing and dance around the bonfire that every village and neighborhood builds. At midnight, country and city folk alike hunt for an elusive (and fictional) fern blossom, ducking into barns and hoping to hear the animals talk. Magical things happen at solstice. From flowers and fine oak branches, revelers weave wreaths to wear on their heads and then float them across lakes in early morning hours.

None of that took place in 1941. That year, as midsummer approached, rumors of impending mass deportations had been circulating for weeks. Like many war veterans, politicians, and police officers, Anthony went into hiding. For added safety, he and his wife agreed to send the children to Ona's parents' farm. Only four kilometers from East Prussia, the farm lay in a restricted zone, adjacent to the German border. Only authorized military personnel and locals were allowed to move in and out of the territory freely, but Ona and Anthony's children, as minors, required no official papers and could enter with their aunt, who came to Kaunas to collect them.

According to the version of events that I was told when I was a child, my grandparents were in the process of moving when Ona's sister arrived for the children. Anthony, the story went, had started a new job in a different city, and Ona had stayed behind in Kaunas to pack up their apartment and prepare for the rest of the family's move. According to every telling of this story that I can remember, it was simply bad luck and an unfortunate coincidence that she came to be alone on that June night.

But on a recent visit to Lithuania, a conversation with a distant female relative who is connected to me via two sets of marriages disturbed my understanding of what happened to my grandmother—and, by extension, to our family—in 1941. I was sitting at this woman's kitchen table, drinking coffee, eating fresh farm cheese, and chatting, when she suggested that it had been no accident that Ona had been home alone the night the soldiers came. My grandfather, it seems, may not have been away purely by coincidence. Instead, warned of impending deportations, he had consciously gone into hiding. They had sent their children to the family farm not simply to get fresh air but for their safety, and Ona was home alone by design.

"Why would she have stayed there?" I asked, incredulous. "Why wouldn't she have gone away as well?" Suddenly I understood that if this version of events was true, it meant that Ona's deportation had been no random stroke of bad luck.

My relative looked uncomfortable at my question but answered gently, "I think she was left behind to protect their belongings. She told me they'd never imagined that they'd take a woman alone." She then added a sentence I've heard countless times over the course of my life but that now took on new meaning: "When she returned from Siberia, Ona told us that she didn't blame Anthony for anything. He had raised their three children, and he'd protected them. For that she would always be grateful."

Anthony and Ona, I saw for the first time, had made a colossal and tragic miscalculation. They had decided to put the mother of their children in the apartment and to bet on the humanity of the arresting soldiers. That gamble turned out to be a poor one, and the repercussions of their decision have reverberated through three generations already.

Though deportations of "anti-Soviet elements" from Lithuania had begun as early as 1940, the first year of Soviet occupation, these actions stepped up dramatically in mid-May 1941. That month, Stalin and Lavrenty Beria, the head of the NKVD (Soviet secret police) from 1938 to 1953, issued a decree ordering the exile of "socially dangerous" elements. Lithuanians call this period of deportations—from June

14 to 19, 1941—"Terrible June." Over six successive nights, Red Army soldiers forcibly removed between 17,500 and 21,000 Lithuanian citizens (5,500 of them children) from their homes, loaded them into cattle cars, and shipped them east. During the same period, approximately 15,000 Latvian citizens were deported from their country. Smaller numbers—around 10,000—were exiled from Estonia. Similar actions had taken place in Belarus and Moldova in preceding months.

The measures targeted business people; bankers; politicians; priests; teachers; professors; landowners; military personnel; police officers; members of national, cultural, and nationalist organizations; and others. The aim of the action was not genocidal. The Soviets were not trying to wipe out an entire people; rather, it was removing its intellectual, political, military, spiritual, and financial leadership, since a leaderless country is more easily occupied and controlled. Most of Lithuania's 17,500–21,000 deportees were ethnic Lithuanians, though not all of them were. Despite a widespread belief among Lithuanians that Jews had largely been at the helm of Bolshevik repression in their country, between 2,000 and 3,000 Jews (or between 8 and 12.5 percent of the deportees)—many of them Bundists or business owners—found themselves forcibly exiled. Given the horrors to come under German occupation, Siberian deportation turned out to be an unexpected salvation for some Jewish exiles.

Historians have now discovered that the Soviet administration had registered 320,000 Lithuanian citizens, along with their families, as deportation targets. This means that had the German invasion not cut the operation short, about half the country's citizens would have landed in Siberia.

7

And so it happened that Ona was alone at 19 Skirgailos Street in Kaunas on the night of June 14, 1941. Normally, four and sometimes five people lived in the Spartan apartment that comprised two rooms, plus a diminutive kitchen, bathroom, and entry hall. She was sleeping when three men (a troika) knocked at the door. It was two o'clock in the morning.

"Papers."

She showed her identity documents.

"Your family."

"Gone," she said, "on vacation."

"Your husband."

"Who knows?" my grandmother answered.

All over Lithuania, similar scenes played out as soldiers knocked on doors, ordered people to pack, and took them away. Despite advance warning and rumors, some deportees were still surprised when the soldiers came for them. Flustered, they grabbed sentimental and useless belongings such as fancy shoes or finely milled hats in panic and ignorance of where they were going and for how long. A remarkable minority had foreseen these events and had made the decision not to run. They prepared carefully and waited calmly. The wisest thought to gather food, linens, and dishes. The most unfortunate traveled almost empty-handed, ending up in permafrost regions with only the clothes on their backs.

Among the deportees were newborns, pregnant women, small children, adolescents, and elderly people. Some would eventually make it back to Lithuania but only after years and even decades in exile. Many lie buried in the Siberian tundra today.

The soldiers gave Ona twenty minutes to prepare. She could take what she could carry. They told her the state would confiscate the rest.

"Your husband will join you at the station," they said. Among her things she folded up Anthony's suit of fine English wool. What else she packed, I don't know. The suit is the only thing she ever named.

I have read stories of men who came out of hiding and joined their wives at the station upon hearing their families had been arrested. They surrendered, hoping to protect their loved ones somehow or to broker an exchange and secure their release. As far as I know, this tactic never worked. Men arrested with their families were separated out and loaded onto trains bound for the Gulag, Stalin's forced labor camp system. Those who gave themselves up later were either shot or arrested on the spot, their families still deported regardless of the sacrifice.

As was the case in earlier centuries, the Stalinist penal system was starkly gendered: the so-called special settlements (which remained a Soviet state secret until the 1990s) were overwhelmingly female spaces. Special settlements were not prisons but farming, fishing, or logging communities, where exiles were made to work. There, people most often lived in family units, and children attended schools. Conditions were harsh, food was scarce, and special settlers had no right to leave their place of registration. Even visiting a neighboring village required official permission. Besides meager rations, they received no pay for their work. Even so, special settlers had a good chance of survival.

The Gulags, meanwhile, were largely male (in 1939–42, women

only made up between 8 and 13 percent of the Gulag population).
Labor camps housed criminals as well as political prisoners. They
had extremely high mortality rates.

Had Anthony been arrested, he would have either been shot on
the spot or sent to a Gulag to do hard labor. But he did not come
out of hiding to meet Ona at the station. Twenty-five years would
pass before she saw him again. Only his finest suit traveled with
her, and it was she who wore it in the mud and snow on the fields
of western Siberia.

At the time of her exile, Ona's youngest child, my father, was six
years old. The middle child, a sister, was ten. The elder sister was
twelve. In an attempt to protect them, Ona signed a statement relin-
quishing her maternal rights on the day of her arrest. The soldiers
must have collected the paper and turned it over to authorities.
Today, it remains filed in the Lithuanian State Historical Archives
among her deportation papers.

Dated June 14, 1941, the statement reads:

> To: The Lithuanian Soviet Socialist People's Security Commission
> I request that my children, currently residing at my mother's farm,
> be allowed to remain with her, in her care, as is presently the case.

On June 16, 1941, two days after Ona signed away her children,
Anthony caught a train back to Kaunas to check on his wife. As
he approached the apartment, he met a neighbor working in the
garden. "God help you," he said to her, offering a traditional blessing
that aims to lighten the burden of those who work the land. She
looked up at him and turned pale.

"Oh, Jesus, Anthony," she said.

The neighbor made sure that the soldier who had been left behind
to wait was no longer upstairs before Anthony entered the apartment himself. Drawers and cupboards stood open, with clothes
and linens spilling out. The place had been ransacked.

Ona's files from the Soviet Ministry of the Interior include an
inventory of items the soldiers seized:

FIG. 4. Ona's children, 1938. Private collection. Courtesy of the author.

1. A photo of the leader of Iron Wolf
2. Seven military medals awarded to Anthony for distinguished service
3. Anthony's membership card for the paramilitary organization Šauliai
4. Anthony's membership card for Iron Wolf
5. A family letter
6. Ona's temporary identity card

After surveying the damage, Anthony sent an unsigned telegram to his in-laws'—Ona's parents'—farm in Lithuania's western borderland: "THERE IS NO ONE." He then set out on foot, walking close to a hundred kilometers to join his children.

While studying a map of Kaunas, I learned that Skirgailos Street was one of the early boundaries of the Kovno Ghetto. This meant, I realized with a shudder, that shortly after Anthony's departure, my family's apartment building had been filled with Jews who had likely died later in concentration camps or by mass shooting. How much sorrow had those walls contained? What, I wondered, is the architecture of loss?

FIG. 5. Ona's family land, 1958. Private collection. Courtesy of the author.

FIG. 6. Ona's family farmhouse, 1958. Private collection. Courtesy of the author.

It's difficult to imagine what a man who comes home to find his wife gone must feel. It's even more difficult to contemplate how he lives with the knowledge that she was taken in his place because he had asked her to protect the family home. That they arrested her because of his politics, not hers.

In *The Book of Embraces*, writer Eduardo Galeano contemplates the fate of an Argentinian poet whose children the military took in his place. The military tortured and eventually killed the poet's son. Galeano asks, "How does one survive such a tragedy? That is survive without one's soul being extinguished?" I've often asked the same question about my grandfather. Perhaps, in the end, only his body survived. Maybe his soul did not.

Ona may not have resented her husband for leaving her to face the soldiers alone, but what about him? Did he blame himself?

Anthony and others like him escaped detention and death only because power changed hands so quickly that June. Days after its soldiers took Ona, the Red Army started its retreat from Lithuania. The deportations halted on June 19, 1941. Three days later, on June 22, 1941, the first German bombs hit Vilnius. German soldiers flooded over the East Prussian border and into western Lithuania, where Anthony and his children now lived.

8

Silence organized our family. There was always, for example, a great hush surrounding the years between 1941, the year Ona was deported to Siberia, and 1944, when her husband, Anthony, and their three children fled westward. These years demarcate the Nazi occupation of Lithuania. Anyone telling us children the story of our family history inevitably jumped from Ona's arrest and deportation in 1941 straight to her children's dramatic departure from Lithuania with their father three years later, in 1944. I was almost an adult before I realized that the second event hadn't followed immediately on the heels of the first. Indeed, so total was the silence surrounding the German occupation, and not only in our family, that I was fifteen before I realized that the Holocaust had anything to do with Lithuania.

From 1941 to 1944, countless atrocities were committed in my grandparents' and parents' country of birth. Who did what—for example, who oversaw the establishment of ghettos or shot so many thousands of Jews at the edges of pits—remains a subject of deep contention in Lithuania. But the death toll of Lithuania's Jews was staggering, and the violence they suffered was horrific and unprecedented. Trainloads of Jews from Western Europe arrived only to be imprisoned and executed in the Ninth Fort in Kaunas.

After the Soviet retreat, Kaunas was the site of one of the most shadowy events of the Holocaust in Lithuania—a massacre perpetrated in an urban garage on June 27, 1941. Lithuanians—though their exact identities remain deeply contested—publicly tortured, beat, and killed several dozen Jewish men. Photographs of the incident exist; however, conspiracy theorists claim they have been doctored.

A number of survivors maintain that the killers were members of a short-lived (1940–41) resistance organization, the Lithuanian Activist Front (LAF), and that they acted not on orders but on their own impulses. According to historian Saulius Sužiedėlis, no conclusive evidence exists to support this claim, though he concedes that the anti-Semitism of the LAF was well known. The organization envisioned its version of the "new Lithuania" as a "one-party anti-Semitic nationalist dictatorship with a single leader (*vadas*) who would guide a disciplined, ethnically and culturally monolithic nation to a new future under the overall guidance of Greater Germany." What's more, Iron Wolf (Anthony's group), which operated within the LAF, envisioned a racially exclusive "Aryan" Lithuanian state.

In August and September 1941, German authorities established two major ghettos—one in Vilnius (Vilna) and one in Kaunas (Kovno)—and then liquidated them in September 1943 and July 1944, respectively. On the outskirts of Vilnius, in the forest of Paneriai (Ponar), today you can visit memorials that mark the mass graves where at least 70,000 Jews were killed between 1941 and 1943, most of whom were prisoners of the Vilnius (Vilna) Ghetto. Another 20,000 Poles and 8,000 Russians lie buried there as well. Shadows of smaller killing sites dot the countryside. By the time the Red Army returned in 1944, more than 90 percent of Lithuania's Jewish community (250,000 in 1939, including those from the Vilnius region and some 12,000 refugees from Poland) had been annihilated.

In late June 1941, having abandoned the ransacked Kaunas apartment, Anthony arrived at his in-laws' farm to find the Bolsheviks gone and his children safe with their grandparents. There, in the country, the family had food to eat and clean water to drink. What's more, there was no immediate threat to them under the Germans. Once the children enrolled in school, Anthony began to search for work again and looked up an old friend, a border guard he used to take target shooting. In late August or early September 1941, he began a job as municipal police chief in the border city of Newtown, the same place he had helped man an emigration point only a few months before.

But while for Anthony, regime change meant salvation from deportation or death, for many thousands of Lithuanian Jews it signified doom. Newtown would be no exception. By the end of 1944, of more than a thousand Jews who lived in the city, only fifteen would survive.

9

We know a lot about the major ghettos of Lithuania, especially about the Vilnius (Vilna) Ghetto. Herman Kruk, that ghetto's librarian, left a long and detailed chronicle of life there, *The Last Days of Jerusalem of Lithuania*. The book details the ghetto inhabitants' reading habits, theater productions, and literary evenings and the trade schools and courts they established. From survivors' accounts, we know about the people's failed uprising and their final days before the ghetto's liquidation. From published diaries such as Avraham Tory's *Surviving the Holocaust*, we know the names, faces, and personalities of the victims of Kaunas and the Kovno Ghetto too.

By contrast, we have a far less complete picture of the experiences of Jews in small Lithuanian towns, in villages, and in the countryside. Unlike the ghettos of Vilnius and Kaunas, the Jews of Lithuania's provinces left a scant record of their suffering—not because they lacked the skills to do so but because they had no time. Whereas the largest urban ghettos of Lithuania lasted until 1943 and 1944, the vast majority of Lithuania's provincial Jews were dead by the end of September 1941, only three short months after the German invasion.

That summer and fall of 1941, when most of Lithuania's Jews died, gas chambers and crematoriums were not yet part of the landscape of German-occupied territory. Unlike later, in the more mechanized stages of the Holocaust, where long, distancing chains of command gave people the impression of moral cover, Lithuania's killings were direct and personal, and the killers' methods were simple and brutal. Local men—auxiliary police usually wearing white arm bands (Holocaust memoirists and historians use the term *baltaraištis*, meaning simply "white armbander," to designate them)—gathered victims and transported them to killing sites either by truck or, as in the Newtown men's massacre, by foot. Pits usually awaited the victims. Patrick Desbois, a French priest who now leads forensic investigations of similar killings in Ukraine, calls this stage the "Holocaust by bullets."

According to postwar trial documents, the shooters of Lithuanian Jews were almost always local men, ethnic Lithuanians, who were often from the very region where the killings happened. Battalions of auxiliary police were first recruited to control the conquered population and territory but not "to kill all Jews as such." But soon, the volunteers' mandate changed, and by August 1941, the extermination of entire Jewish communities had begun. Local recruits lined victims up in small groups at the edges of pits and shot them in their heads one by one. In places like Newtown, the victims and the killers often knew one another personally. To ease things along, authorities gave the shooters alcohol during such operations, and stories of drunk men returning from such actions singing patriotic songs were legendary among survivors. There are also tales of shooters going mad because of what they saw and did.

In video testimony gathered in the 1990s and early 2000s, Lithuanian eyewitnesses, children at the time, tell of climbing up onto high tree branches to investigate where the gunshots they heard were coming from. They describe horrific scenes of men swinging infants against tree trunks, smashing their skulls, apparently to save bullets. Once everyone was dead, the killers rifled through clothing and packages and pocketed valuables before covering the dead with powdery pine forest earth.

Anthony's KGB file is vague in its time lines. The eyewitness testimony gathered there refers only to "the beginning of the German occupation." With no months or dates to go by in the file, and in the absence of police rosters, we must estimate. According to one source—a Newtown historian named Romas—Anthony took the job of police chief in late August 1941. By then, two major massacres had already taken place in the city. I do not know who was police chief before him or why there was a change in that position.

According to the files, Anthony worked as chief for five months. When I asked, his elder daughter confirmed that this "seemed about right." That would have him leaving the post in January or February 1942.

The first Newtown massacre took place in the early days of the German occupation, or late June 1941, and targeted communists. All men older than fourteen were assembled in the market square and then marched over a bridge and out into fields. There, the men lined up for inspection by a local priest, who selected nine individuals. Eight were to die for being party activists. His tender age didn't save the ninth, a fifteen-year-old Lithuanian boy named Vincas Kinka, the leader of the ubiquitous Soviet youth group called the Pioneers. The auxiliary police marched him, together with the eight other chosen men, to the Jewish cemetery to be shot. Today, a gravestone stands for each of those nine victims. It surprised me to learn that not a single Jew was killed that day.

Locals refer to what took place next, sometime between July 4 and 10, 1941, as the "men's massacre." Most of what we know about these killings comes from Newtown's Glick family.

Until 1940 like the vast majority of their Christian neighbors, the Glicks were farmers. The youngest of their children, seven-year-old Isaac, had attended a Lithuanian kindergarten, where he learned the country's official language in addition to the Yiddish his family spoke at home. On the day I visited him in 2014, we conversed for four hours in Lithuanian. Only one of us spoke with an accent, and it wasn't Isaac Glick. Today, he is the sole surviving member of his family and the last Jew of Newtown. He told me the following story.

On the night of the men's massacre, Lithuanian auxiliary police-men arrived at the town's Jewish homes. They instructed all men older than the age of fourteen to pack clothes and food for a three-day journey to Germany, where they were ostensibly being sent to work. Isaac added that the Lithuanian police officers themselves appeared to believe this cover story, since one of his brothers was excused from the "trip" due to illness and he survived the war as a result. In the end, the men took Isaac's father, grandfather, and eldest brother away to their deaths.

A handful of townswomen and children followed the convoy. Later, they reported what had happened next: The men were marched to a barn near the river and beside the Jewish cemetery, where a mass grave had been prepared. Machine gun shots rang out as the sun set. The Germans walked the perimeter of the barn to keep witnesses away. The shooting continued all night, not ceasing until morning.

Once the sun had risen, Malke Glick, Isaac's mother, decided to venture out and investigate. She took an older daughter and young Isaac along. Buckets in hand, the three made their way over to the municipal grazing site, as if to milk cows. From the field they could see a mound of earth piled beside the pit in the cemetery. A few Jewish men worked to bury the dead as their guards laughed and pissed in the grave. Once they had completed their work, the diggers were shot. In all, 192 men were killed in that massacre.

10

By the time Anthony arrived on the borderland in late August 1941, as in other small places, Newtown's remaining Jews were confined to a so-called open ghetto. Although no walls or barbed wire confined residents, Gentiles were strictly prohibited from frequenting these areas or trading with those who lived there. Jews had no right to leave the open ghetto and move around the city. Jewish businesses had been confiscated and their assets seized. Smaller humiliations also applied: Jews were barred from drinking from the town's water fountain or from using the sidewalks. Auxiliary police could enter Jewish homes unbidden and "borrow" watches, jewelry, and other valuables. Young girls, such as the elder of Isaac's two sisters, were relegated to dirty work like cleaning soldiers' toilets, and doubtless they fell victim to sexual attacks.

G—— was the son of Newtown's pharmacist. Isaac told me that he thought the boy—around nineteen years of age—was sweet on his elder sister Pescia. Fair-haired and pretty, Pescia had worked for the pharmacist before the German occupation. After she lost this job, G—— stayed in contact. In mid-September 1941, the young pharmacist's son came to warn her that another massacre was planned, and he offered to arrange a hiding place for her in the countryside. Pescia refused to leave without her family and stood firm against his attempts to change her mind. Eventually, she prevailed. He agreed to make plans for all five remaining Glicks.

One detail from the Glick family's experience strikes and troubles me: G——, the young man who warned the Glicks of the impending massacre, would later aim his rifle into a pit filled with the bodies of his neighbors.

The massacre was scheduled for dawn on the morning of September 16, 1941. As before, Newtown's Jewish women and their children were told to prepare for travel to Germany, where they would join their husbands. No one would listen to Malke Glick, Isaac's mother, when she warned them of what was to come. No one believed her when she told the women that, in truth, their husbands, sons, and fathers lay buried in the ground. Instead, the women packed their things for the journey.

Heavily armed guards loaded them into trucks. A man named Vyšniauskas claims that "he was forced to drive a carriage full of Jewish women and children" to the Paražniai (Parazhnever, in Yiddish) Forest. This driver took them not over the river but rather six kilometers outside the town and into the forest, where a mass grave awaited.

Before dawn on the morning of the massacre, Isaac and his mother, Malke, escaped death by wading over a sandbar in the river. A farmer named Vaičiūnas met them and hid the two in his barn, where Malke's other children awaited, having traveled there separately. The farmer gave them strict instructions not to come out for anyone but him. G—— was dangerous, he warned, and not to be trusted.

He was right. After the shootings, the pharmacist's son returned to the barn, drunk. He crashed around, rifle in hand, demanding that the Glicks come out and show themselves. Forewarned, they remained hidden. No doubt, the farmer's prescience saved the family.

When night fell, the Glicks split up and went out into the countryside. For months, Isaac and Malke were handed off from farmer to farmer. When he tells his story, Isaac calls it a relay race. Out on

FIG. 7. Isaac Glick, 2014. Photo by the author.

the land surrounding Newtown, five members of the Glick family, including little Isaac, survived with the help of local families.

Ultimately, Isaac's mother found him a place in a monastery, where he lived under a pseudonym while posing as an orphan. He stayed there for close to three years, long enough for his mother to become a hazy memory. When the war ended, the woman who arrived to collect him seemed only vaguely familiar. Isaac's mother and three siblings survived. That was more than seventy years ago. Today, of his entire family—indeed, of the entire Jewish community of Newtown—only Isaac Glick remains.

11

A few blocks past Newtown's market square, a road sign indicates, "Jewish Cemetery: Mass Graves." Beyond an iron gate adorned with a Star of David lie old gravestones bearing Hebrew letters. Most are broken. Wildflowers bloom all around. I crouch before the monument to the Jewish dead, leave a fieldstone at its foot, and slip another fieldstone into my pocket to take home.

Across the river, just beyond the graves, scant traces of the formerly Prussian city of Schirwindt and its architectural jewel remain. A cathedral modeled after Cologne's famous Dom once rose from its town center. In 1944 and 1945, with no border separating the two cities, Lithuanians (and others, the person who told me this story hastened to add) were free to cross into East Prussia and take what they needed. Though the cathedral survived most of World War II unharmed, once Schirwindt found itself inside the Soviet zone in 1944, Newtowners traversed the bridge and dismantled the edifice brick by brick. They looted and carried away its components to rebuild their devastated city. Today, Schirwindt has been renamed Kutuzovo. It looks as it did immediately after the war, being almost entirely uninhabited. Only part of the former school still stands, functioning as a barracks for border guards.

In addition to the cathedral's parts, Newtowners used Jewish headstones to restore and repair their buildings' foundations, and

FIG. 8. A prewar view of Schirwindt from Newtown. The cathedral can be seen in the distance. The Scheschuppe River separates the two cities, no date. Private collection. Courtesy of Romas Treideris.

FIG. 9. The broken gravestones of Newtown's Jewish cemetery, 2014. Photo by the author.

that is why so many are broken or missing from the cemetery today. Such was the practice all over Lithuania. I first heard about the use of Jewish headstones as building materials when I was a teenager, but back then I didn't believe it. The story seemed too callous to be true.

No, impossible, I thought, recalling the "cemetery visiting days" of my childhood. We prepared for the occasion days in advance, trimming bushes, planting flowers, and placing candles around the headstones of our departed loved ones. On cemetery visiting day, the parish celebrated Mass outdoors among the dead. *Lithuanians take their cemeteries far too seriously for such desecration to be true,* I concluded, and I decided the story of the headstones had to be a tasteless legend. I was wrong.

12

The Lithuanian history I learned in Saturday language school never mentioned these events, for perhaps obvious reasons. To talk about the mass killing of Jews, one must also address mass passivity and collaboration during the Nazi occupation. For a community that defines itself first and foremost as a victim of illegal and repressive Soviet occupation, this is, to say the least, uncomfortable. It's also not the kind of story that any community wants to tell its children about their grandparents' generation.

There were, of course, some Lithuanian rescuers—people we now call righteous among the nations—but the numbers speak for themselves. When more than 90 percent of a community (the prewar Lithuanian Jewish population numbered 160,000) was killed, how effective could the resistance have been? I suspect that even young children can make that calculation.

But silence didn't reign only in the West. The homegrown Holocaust—or Catastrophe, as it was called in the USSR—also went undiscussed in Soviet Lithuania, although the reasons for that particular silence differed. Postwar Soviet historiography initially distorted and even suppressed Holocaust scholarship and remembrance largely on idiosyncratic grounds—specifically, due to Stalin's sudden and rabid anti-Semitism, which reached a fever pitch in 1948 and 1949. Over those two years, authorities launched a campaign to destroy Soviet Jewish culture. Jewish museums—including one in

Vilnius—and other cultural institutions were forced to close their doors. After the war, Stalin saw Zionist plots all around, despite the large numbers of Jews in his family and among his advisers. On August 12–13, 1952, the tyrant had thirteen prominent Soviet Yiddish writers executed for no discernable reason beyond his paranoia toward Jews.

But the subject of the Holocaust remained taboo in the Soviet Union even after the dictator's 1953 demise. When authorities did mark and commemorate massacres, they generally overlooked the victims' Jewish identities. Even today, visitors to Lithuania find Soviet-era monuments that mention the deaths only of "Soviet citizens," not of Jews. A few exceptions from that time include the publication of G. Erslavaitė and others' *Masinės žudynės Lietuvoje* (Mass killings in Lithuania) (1965), a handful of books on the Ninth Fort and Soviet Jewish partisans, and Sofia Binkienė's *Ir be ginklo kariai* (Soldiers without weapons) (1967) about rescuers.

Soviet schoolchildren grew up with the narrative of the Great Patriotic War fought against fascism and for the ideal of friendship among the nations. Russification was strongly enforced in non-Russian-speaking republics, and conformity was the order of the day. Ideology did not permit Jewish lives to be treated as different or special, as all were Soviet citizens. The same was thus true of Jewish deaths; they too were Soviet. Collective memory folded Holocaust victims into the grand total of Soviet war losses. In fact, the number of Jews killed by the Germans in the USSR—1 million native-born Soviet Jews, plus 1.6 million Polish, Lithuanian, and Latvian Jews brought into the fold by the 1939 and 1940 Soviet annexations—long remained a Soviet state secret.

Professional Western historians, for their part, have written little about small and marginal places like Newtown because for decades the documents necessary to do this kind of work remained inaccessible. Locked in special archives behind the Iron Curtain, files such as Anthony's were guarded by select teams of clerks who had high enough security clearance to work with classified records. Few Soviet historians would have been allowed unencumbered use of postwar trial documents and of search files containing eyewitness testimonies from Soviet war crimes investigations conducted in the 1940s and '50s. Oral history too would have been near impossible to gather. Before the 1990s, eyewitnesses would have rarely dared to speak to Western researchers for fear of being labeled a spy. Today this has changed. Since regaining its independence in 1990, Lithuania has been open for more than twenty-six years.

Fortunately, when the Soviet Union fell, it did so without erasing all its traces. Change happened so quickly that the regime's archivists managed to destroy only the inventories and the finding aids to their collections but not the files themselves. In 2006 after some discussion as to how and whether to control access to information that was potentially both damning and illuminating, Lithuanian authorities decided to open KGB and other formerly secret Soviet files to researchers and to the public. Today 95 percent of the KGB documents are available to read. The remaining 5 percent, which include such materials as lists of KGB collaborators, remain classified, though their declassification is up for discussion. Comprising more than 1.2 million files, Lithuania's collection is the largest open repository of KGB records anywhere in the former USSR.

Since the fall of the Soviet Union, thousands of individuals have been able to request their own files and those of their families. Ordinary citizens can read records of how they were watched and why, see informant reports, and, for the first time, get an accurate picture of how the regime viewed them. It is apt that to do so, one must go to the former KGB (and Gestapo) building in Vilnius. Situated on Vilnius's main boulevard, the imposing mint-hued building, whose basement once contained torture chambers, today houses a public archive. When I arrived at the second-floor reading room, it was full of researchers working at small wooden desks. I introduced myself and asked the archivist to bring me everything she could find about Newtown.

KGB "punishment" or trial files all take the same form. They open with a page summarizing the crime in question and lay out the evidence contained in the dossier. Each collection of documents includes the length and nature of the court's imposed sentence, followed by a short declaration listing the convict's property to be confiscated. There are countless pages of interview transcripts on onionskin paper, tiny photographs tucked into envelopes, signed confessions, and even the occasional prison diary. All the files bear cover stamps declaring them "Top Secret." Most of the contents are in Russian, though, on occasion, I have come across witness statements in Lithuanian.

The KGB files that I read at one of those little wooden desks attest that after the war, Soviet courts tried some of the Newtown shooters. I counted nine convictions in the documents I examined in Vilnius. Some of the files came from war tribunals that took place in 1948 and 1949. Other convictions were handed down as late as 1955. Each of those convicted received a sentence of hard labor in the Siberian Gulag. I imagine few of the men (all the shooters were men) survived to return home.

From these documents, it's hard to imagine what the trials were like. There is no indication of whether observers were present in the court, as there were, for example, in Nuremberg. There are no photographs of the courtroom, no traces of judges' personalities. Only a weirdly scrapbook-style bureaucracy.

Those named in the Newtown shooters' files include a man named Bergeris, who was described to me as a sadist who committed suicide at the end of the German occupation. Trial documents name two men named Gudiškis and Milašauskas as having received twenty years' hard labor each. A man called Slusčius got ten years for leading Jews to a massacre site and confiscating belongings. Another, Šventuraitis, received five years for arresting both Jews and communists. In addition to the nine "punishment files" of the convicted, I found eleven search files. Each accuses a separate man of collaborating with the Germans and then escaping to the West to avoid prosecution.

Anthony's file is among them.

Soviet-era records such as those documenting Anthony's wartime employment are treated with deep suspicion in the former USSR and in émigré communities like the one in Toronto where I grew up. Any Soviet-era evidence or testimony is dismissed as tainted and unreliable, and the notion of Soviet justice is considered an oxymoron. Undeniably, there was an element of propaganda to Soviet war crimes trials both under Stalin, until 1953, and in the 1960s and 1970s. One purpose of such trials of war criminals in the USSR was to attack both foreign and domestic enemies. No serious historian appears to dispute this point. For this reason, we are right to be suspicious of such KGB files and court records.

Still, the historians I consulted—experts in the region and of the period—told me that these documents were nonetheless worthy of attention. "They can be useful, sometimes critically important," read one response to my email query, "but are always to be utilized with caution." The historian added, "Some documents are indeed unreliable." Even so, the reply continued, "*that does not mean that the entire collection can be dismissed.*"

Lithuanian authorities chose not to heed that historian's warning. Beginning in 1989, they wasted no time in vacating Soviet convictions as soon as possible. The state quickly issued fifty thousand pardons to citizens who had been found guilty of resisting occupation regimes in the past decades. Among these thousands were artists, religious dissidents, and political activists. Predictably, a number of people convicted of killing Jews during the Nazi occupation were also among the pardoned. Lithuanian authorities tried to rectify this by adding to the law a 1990 clause that forbade pardoning "anyone who had been involved in killings or acts of genocide." By 1998 the state had revoked twenty-two pardons, but international controversy persists.

13

When I first read the accusations against my grandfather, I sat at my desk for weeks, turning them in my head. Closing my eyes, I imagined gunshots and struggled to conceive of what three hundred or four hundred of them in succession would sound like, but my mind couldn't get past the first three or four. By the fifth burst, I felt panic rising and had to open my eyes, reach out, and hang onto something solid.

Lithuanian archivists have told me that the records dating from the German occupation are spotty, because so much burned in the wartime bombings. And though some municipal police rosters still exist, I found none for Newtown.

Oral history is the next best thing to documentary evidence.

"Your grandfather was my father's good friend," said Romas, a Newtown historian, over tea and cake in his Vilnius apartment. Romas is the son of Anthony's target-shooting friend, the one my grandfather looked up when he needed a job in 1941. I found him more or less by chance when I went into the Šakiai public library to consult its librarians. I told them my story and asked a few questions about the region. Within half an hour, they had Romas on the phone and were arranging for us to meet.

Romas continued, "They worked together, first as border guards and then as police officers. Anthony used to come to our house for lunch when he was police chief. I used to hide and eavesdrop on their conversations. I was ten years old."

Romas was as stunned to meet me, it seemed, as I was surprised to have found him. It took us some time to get to the war and Anthony's regular visits to his home, since he wanted to know everything about our family: what had happened to Ona and her children, how many grandchildren she'd had, and what had brought me to Lithuania.

Over the preceding decades, he had amassed an impressive collection of vintage photographs and maps of Newtown. Among them were nineteenth-century postcards and innocuous street scenes, but he had also found Nazi-era images. I flipped silently through the photographs. They showed German officers in Schutzstaffel (SS) uniforms celebrating the New Year, a German customs officer flanked by the coats of arms of the Third Reich and the Republic of Lithuania, Soviet prisoners of war (POWs) building their barracks, and a wide shot of a swastika-emblazoned flag flying over Newtown.

Finally, after a long discussion, Romas and I made our way to the subject of the German occupation, to Anthony's tenure as police chief, and to the massacre that happened on my grandfather's watch. At dawn on September 16, 1941, after Malke Glick and her children had slipped away, the remaining Jewish women and children of Newtown were loaded into trucks and carriages and driven into the Paražniai Forest. The KGB files say 300–400 people were killed that day, but estimates have risen since their compilation. Historian Arūnas Bubnys more recently put the number of victims at 650. *The Holocaust Atlas of Lithuania* cites up to 700 dead.

A few days earlier in Newtown, two city museum workers had drawn on memory and on local knowledge to help me find the mass grave. As we drove, the road had grown both rougher and softer. Eventually, we'd abandoned the car and walked to the forest's edge. Mosquitoes quickly blanketed my jeans, and a layer of dusty soil covered my boots.

A few hundred meters down the trail, I spotted a pyramid-shaped

FIG. 10. German officers celebrating the New Year in Newtown, no date. Private collection. Courtesy of Romas Treideris.

FIG. 11. A German customs officer on the bridge between Schirwindt and Newtown, no date. Private collection. Courtesy of Romas Treideris.

FIG. 12. Soviet POWs building their prison camp in Newtown, 1941. Private collection. Courtesy of Romas Treideris.

FIG. 13. Soviet POWs constructing their barracks at Oflag 60 in Newtown, 1941. Private collection. Courtesy of Romas Treideris.

FIG. 14. The swastika flying over Newtown, no date. Private collection. Courtesy of Romas Treideris.

FIG. 15. Monument to the Jewish women and children of Newtown, 2014. Photo by the author.

and moss-covered cairn. It marked a depression ringed by small boulders. Inside the stone perimeter grew ferns, grasses, and tiny evergreens.

Beneath them lay the town's Jewish women and children.

I walked slowly around the site, taking care to photograph it from

FIG. 16. The killing site in Paražniai Forest, 2014. Photo by the author.

all angles. I said a prayer. *I'm sorry*, I said. I said it again. And again. The phrase echoed inside me. My breath quickened. These were the killings that Anthony had overseen as police chief.

"My mother was so angry at him," Romas said, snapping me back from the memory of the gravesite and to the present. He took a sip of tea. "I heard her yelling at Anthony on the day after the women and children were shot. She accused him of murder. But he defended himself. He said he hadn't gone to the forest, but that he'd stayed in his office. 'I didn't shoot anyone,' he said."

Romas looked at me, dead serious, and repeated this. He put down his teacup. "Your grandfather didn't shoot anyone."

Doubt and ambivalence immobilized me. Stone-faced, I looked at him.

He said it, in part, because he knew I had papers that suggested otherwise.

14

Besides Malke Glick and her children, I know of two additional survivors of Newtown.

The first, Mira Rosenfeld, a girl of perhaps ten years of age, emerged from under the dead of the September 16 women's and children's massacre and returned to Newtown on foot. A wealthy Lithuanian named Jonynas took her in and adopted her as his own. Since he was friendly with local police and had been persecuted by the Bolsheviks, Jonynas did not fear for his safety under the German regime. The man baptized and renamed the girl Rasa, believing both his social status and her new Catholic identity would protect her. It did, for a time.

The second survivor was Dr. Isaac Grossman. Already elderly in 1941—around eighty-two years of age—the doctor had long lived in Newtown and was likely a native of the city. He offered medical care to the town's citizens and those of the surrounding villages regardless of ethnicity or economic circumstance. Why or how Dr. Grossman received a reprieve from the roundup and cemetery shooting of Jewish men is unclear, but he survived the men's massacre. Later, when again he was to be killed with the women and children, Newtowners organized a petition asking the German occupiers to spare his life once more. That too worked. For a time.

Toward the end of the war, in 1944, authorities summoned Jonynas and Mira for document inspection. The girl, they told Jonynas, had to go "to Germany." Soldiers took her into custody. They shot her in one of the region's many forests some kilometers outside of town. Though probably not on the same day or in the same forest, Dr. Grossman suffered the same fate.

Anthony's search file contains one very specific allegation regarding these events. In August 1947, a man named M—— told a Soviet investigator that Anthony had shot Dr. Grossman. The testimony offered was secondhand; that is, M—— did not claim to have seen the killing but that someone else had told him of it.

More than anything else, this—the specific accusation that Anthony had personally killed Dr. Grossman—was the piece of the puzzle that had brought me to Lithuania. At home, at my desk, Dr. Grossman's was the only name I'd had. He was the only specific victim, and this fact obsessed me. I needed to find out who Dr. Grossman had been and if Anthony's was the last face he ever saw.

"The archival documents say that he shot Dr. Grossman," I finally said to Romas after a long silence.

"No," he shook his head. "That's not true. Germans shot Dr. Grossman in the Kataučizna Forest. He was killed in retaliation for the murder of a German in a village not far from Newtown."

It was Romas's turn to pause. He sighed.

"Anthony got stuck," he continued. "He couldn't refuse. He had a family to protect."

I remained still for a minute or two. "You told me the mayor quit after the shootings began because he wanted no part of it. Nothing happened to him. You said your father hid in the countryside when Anthony told him to come and round up Jews."

"Yes," said Romas.

"So it was possible to refuse." I felt my voice shake as I said this.

"Yes," he answered. "I suppose it was."

FIG. 17. The first photograph of Dr. Grossman, no date. Private collection. Courtesy of Romas Treideris.

Before I left his apartment, Romas gave me two photographs of Dr. Grossman. Back at my hotel, I lay on my bed and studied the images for a long time. I tried to discern who this man had been and strained to reach across the yawning gulf that separated us. In the first, the balding doctor stands behind a table atop a set of stone stairs. He squints against the sun. To his right stands a woman in a hat; to the left, three other men in suits. Vases adorn the table placed before them, and children watch the ceremony from below. I don't know what they are celebrating. Perhaps it is Independence Day or a war commemoration. Maybe it is the official opening of the museum I visited in Newtown.

In my imagination, I hear Dr. Grossman address the citizens gathered before him. He speaks with a lilting Yiddish accent. With no side locks or yarmulke, he would have carried his Jewishness primarily on his tongue. I know he was unmarried; Romas told me so. I wondered as I studied his face if he kept kosher, if he went to synagogue, if he believed in God.

It's clear from the second photograph, dated June 1921, that Dr. Grossman was not only shorter and heavier than the men

FIG. 18. The second photograph of Dr. Grossman (first on the right, second row), 1921. Private collection. Courtesy of Romas Treideris.

surrounding him but also older. He had a mustache. He dressed smartly. I find his rumpled suit endearing.

An educator, a healer, and a member of the city council, Dr. Grossman was engaged in civic life. He interacted closely with the non-Jewish Lithuanians of his town and spoke their language fluently. It was his job, more than one person told me as I made my way around his home city of Newtown, to inspect the health of Lithuanian troops stationed in the city.

Ultimately, the KGB files accuse Anthony not of executing mass killing but of oversight and coordination. Romas, it seems, was right. My grandfather almost certainly did not kill Dr. Grossman. The first detail that doesn't match up is the timing of the doctor's murder. In 1944, when the physician and Mira perished, Anthony was no longer working as police chief.

Second, a number of witnesses claim unequivocally that it was a German who shot Dr. Grossman, as Romas told me, and that it was done in retaliation for the killing of a German soldier in a nearby hamlet. What's more, I have read in numerous accounts that Dr. Grossman's killer wore a German uniform.

When I asked him during our second meeting a few days later, Romas confirmed that Lithuanian auxiliary police did not wear German uniforms. In Newtown, he said, Anthony and the other city police had donned their old border guard uniforms. Eyewitnesses from the KGB files say so too.

"Would it have been possible to mix them up? To mistake a Lithuanian for a German?" I asked.

"No," Romas replied. "Impossible."

Small consolation. In fact, it's no consolation at all. Anthony may not have been a killer, but he was an intermediary who received orders from on high and passed them on to the shooters below him. On that day he retreated to his office while his subordinates gunned people down in forests because he told them to do it. What innocence can be afforded such a chief?

And regardless of who pulled the trigger and when, both Dr. Grossman and Mira Rosenfeld died terrible deaths.

Since my conversations with Romas, I've thought a lot about what Anthony's crime—his wartime collaboration—means for me as his granddaughter. Thus far, I've come up with no good answers.

Am I guilty too in some way, either genetically or by inheritance? I don't think so.

Do I have a responsibility to the dead: to Dr. Grossman, to Mira Rosenfeld, to my grandmother Ona?

Yes, I believe so.

My task is both writerly and simply human: to tell the truth as best I can. To accept what happened without justifying murder and without comparing pain.

Not everyone is on board with this project.

The times were complicated, say my elders.

You are too young to understand.

You weren't there. You don't know.

Perhaps.

Still, again and again, the same questions return: What justification exists for gunning down children in forests? For killing their mothers as the children watch? For stealing fathers, grandfathers, and brothers and then taking them to their deaths? What credible defense can be offered for taking the life of an elderly doctor? Of an adolescent girl?

The only possible answer is none. None at all.

15

Lithuanian "Jew-shooters" (*žydšaudžiai*), as they are called, were not card-carrying Nazis. Nor were they easily recognizable monsters. On the contrary, they were ordinary, local men who followed the call of the provisional government (secretly formed in April 1941 and dissolved in August the same year) for officials who had held office before June 15, 1940, to return to their posts. Others were citizens who had risen up against the first Soviet occupation in June 1941, when the provisional government was officially confirmed. Eventually, once German rule had been established, these men were grouped in precincts and became local police forces. Members of these local forces, along with volunteers (like G——, the Newtown pharmacist's son), ultimately became "Jew-shooters."

In my conversations with Isaac Glick and other Newtowners who had been children during the war, I found little confusion or disagreement about who did what. All the witnesses recounted the same sequence of events and named similar perpetrators. Everyone agreed, for example, on the number of massacres and that local Lithuanians had done most of the shooting.

My friend L——, who spent his childhood and teenage years in Vilnius, shares an interest in things Litvak and in wartime Lithuania. He also has an insider perspective—the sardonic, almost cynical, worldview of someone raised in the USSR—that is invaluable to me.

This can be good for me as he shakes me out of naive assumptions and forces me to question what I know.

As we talked by phone one autumn day, shortly before my trip to Newtown, our conversation turned to who had known what of the killings of Jews in Lithuania. When I asked him what he thought of the claim that ethnic Lithuanians had no idea what was happening to their Jewish neighbors, L—— scoffed.

"Everyone knew," he said, "who collaborated, who killed, and who saved lives. Everyone knew everything."

To support his assertion, he offered an anecdote.

In the 1980s, L—— had traveled into the Lithuanian countryside with his Vilnius classmates. Those children born in the 1960s and '70s of course had no memory of the Great Patriotic War or, for that matter, of the ghettos of the German occupation. The children's task was ethnographic—to gather folklore and oral history. I imagine my friend was as fearless back then as he is now and that he strolled up to a house, knocked boldly on its door, and engaged its proprietor, an elderly woman, in conversation.

When L—— asked her what sort of people lived in the area, she pointed to the homes around her and replied, "Oh, that's where the postman lives. There's the old farmer's family. And that one there's the Jew-shooter."

"Everyone knew," my friend repeated. "The words rolled off her tongue."

The ordinariness of the Jew-shooters may seem obvious now, some five decades after Hannah Arendt coined the phrase "the banality of evil." Her book *Eichmann in Jerusalem* (1963) tells the story of the trial of Adolf Eichmann, a high-level Nazi military officer and bureaucrat who facilitated and oversaw the logistics of the mass deportation of Jews to ghettos and extermination camps. In 1960 Israeli Mossad agents captured him near his Buenos Aires home and brought him to Israel, where he stood trial for war crimes and crimes against humanity. Convicted on numerous counts, Eichmann was hanged in 1962.

In her book and in the series of *New Yorker* articles that preceded it, Arendt portrayed Eichmann as a petty bureaucrat whose deeds were monstrous but who himself was "ordinary" and "commonplace." The portrait sparked a furious controversy. I think the notion that a seemingly normal human being could take part in and even organize mass murder was offensive to many because it raised the possibility that any one of us, given the wrong circumstances, could find ourselves party to such crimes.

Stanley Milgram, an American psychologist, decided to test this hypothesis. He wanted to know how far regular people would go and how much pain they might inflict on a stranger just because an authority figure told them to do it. Three people took part in each of his experiments: a learner, a teacher, and an experimenter (that is, Milgram himself). The experimenter instructed the teacher to administer electric shocks to the learner whenever he made an error in matching word pairs. The true focus of the experiment was, of course, the teacher.

The results surprised even Milgram. A sizable majority (twenty-six of forty) obeyed the experimenter and delivered what they believed to be the generator's most powerful shock. This ultimate shock, had it been real, would have been fatal.

He repeated the experiment a number of times. In the first variant, as described earlier, the teachers could not see their learners. They heard only (prerecorded) cries of pain and protest. But in a second variant, where the teacher could see the learner, compliance with the demands of the authority (the experimenter) declined significantly. In a third, where the teacher was required to hold a learner's hand to a shock plate, even fewer teachers obeyed. Proximity to the victim reduced their obedience. This revelation led Milgram to think about the power structures that, he hypothesized, had allowed for killing on such a massive scale. By concentrating on their role in the chain of command, perpetrators could blind themselves to the consequences of their actions.

In his analysis of the results, Milgram homed in on three terms to reevaluate: loyalty, duty, and discipline. Importantly, at least for my thinking about Anthony's actions, we extol these qualities as military virtues. "They refer not to the 'goodness' of the person per se," writes Milgram, "but to the adequacy with which a subordinate fulfills his socially defined role. The loyal soldier, in this line of thinking, is responsible only for carrying out orders. The responsibility for the orders themselves lies elsewhere." Perhaps then, Milgram suggests, such military "virtues" are not virtuous at all. Perhaps, loyalty, duty, obedience, and discipline are characteristics our society should eradicate.

I believe that a great number of those Lithuanians who collaborated in the killing of more than 90 percent of the country's Jewish community were terribly obedient men who had internalized a military ethos. They followed orders at all costs and in a manner that allowed them, at least on the level of personal conscience, to disavow any responsibility for the deaths they caused. "Not I but the system did it in which I was a cog," is how Arendt sums up this line of thinking. *I didn't come up with the idea,* goes the argument, *I was just obeying orders.*

But then Arendt counters that justification: "And why, if you please, did you become a cog or continue to be a cog under such circumstances?" she asks. "No one can force you to kill," she writes. "They can only tempt you to do so." Choosing to be part of a killing machine remains a choice. And death remains the end result, whether arrived at by the hand of one or of a series of individuals; whether committed up close or from afar.

There is a photograph among the many images of my family that is unlike any others. Dated 1923, it shows a handsome young man in a straw flat-topped hat and a three-piece suit. He stands in a garden and holds a thin cane. A hint of a smile sneaks across his face. Affable and even gentle looking, he seems not at all similar to the stern grandfather I knew.

While studying this photograph, an awful, almost unspeakable question enters my mind: Would it have been better for him to be deported that June day too? Had he been taken with Ona, none of the accusations outlined in the KGB files would have existed. He

FIG. 19. Anthony in 1923. Private collection. Courtesy of the author.

would have been far away when the Germans came and when the Jews were shot. He would never have been faced with the choice of whether to become a cog.

In this alternate and, yes, selfish history, where I can change only one fate, Anthony would have been a clear, clean victim. A hero, even. Is it possible that the tragedy wasn't Ona's deportation but her husband's escape?

16

In 1944 before they shot him in the Kataučizna Forest, where his bones now rest, Dr. Grossman turned to his executioners and said, "All my life I have worked for the good of humanity. And for this, I have earned a bullet in the head."

You are remembered, I want to say to him. *You live on*, I want to insist. But, in truth, I am powerless. Impotent. There is nothing I can do to repair the damage. No way to atone for the crimes of the past.

17

By late 1941 and early 1942, Lithuania was fully under German occupation. The vast majority of Jews in the Lithuanian countryside were now dead. Those who remained were either in hiding or imprisoned in urban ghettos and work camps. And in December or January of that winter, Anthony left Newtown and his post as chief of police. He collected his three children from the nearby in-laws' farm and moved them into a second-floor apartment in Šakiai, the city some twenty kilometers east of Newtown, where I had consulted the public librarians. There, Anthony worked as a trade unionist for masons and sawmill workers. What prompted this change in position, I don't know.

According to family lore, moving back to Šakiai was the best thing that Anthony could have done for his daughters and son. There was no food to buy in the stores, but with the grandparents' farm nearby, the family never went hungry. The children attended a school only meters from their doorstep, and life went on, without a hiccup, until July 1944, when the Red Army began once again to draw close to the Lithuanian-Prussian borderland.

Capture by the Soviets could only mean execution or exile for Anthony, so he hitched his in-laws' two best horses to a long grain wagon packed with food and prepared to leave. Though East Prussia lay a mere four kilometers away, just over the Scheschuppe River, the family wasn't able to cross that night. Instead, he and his three children slept in a nearby storehouse and waited for dawn.

Early the next day, Anthony's mother-in-law arrived by horse and wagon. Frightened by reports of difficult conditions in Germany, she begged him not to take the children and to leave them at the farm instead. After consulting his elder daughter, Anthony relented. He sent the two younger children back with their grandmother before heading west over the river alone. The eldest child stayed to see him off, then retraced the four kilometers back to the farm on foot.

When she returned, the daughter found her grandparents' farm overrun. German soldiers had seized the remaining livestock, and the house and barn were full of people ready to flee. Three, maybe four days passed before Anthony returned with a single horse and a smaller wagon. He retrieved his children, leaving his in-laws behind. Ona's mother and youngest sister eventually made their way to the United States as refugees. Ona's eldest sister and brother-in-law would be exiled to Siberia by the Soviets.

Anthony and his children moved through East Prussia, sleeping in ditches and wrapping themselves in a carpet that they eventually took all the way to northern England. But first, they had to make their way through Germany. In Stallupönen, Germany, they slept in barracks and battled bedbugs, which fell from the dark ceiling, until Anthony procured train tickets to Berlin. He had heard that a private factory was looking for workers there.

One summer's day a few years ago now, while my husband and I were in Berlin, I set out on the S-Bahn to see if I could find the former beer hall where Anthony and his children had lived for four months. It was a cool summer day, overcast and gloomy. Transport and construction noise filled the boulevard, but soon enough I'd found it, the modest traditional house standing on a triangular island in the road. Contemplating the building, I stood frozen in the bustle of the sidewalk but felt strangely little by way of emotion or secondhand, inherited recognition. The neighborhood of looming Soviet-style apartment blocks seemed poor.

Having taken in the sight of the beer hall, I then set out to walk the length of Landsberger Allee, noting women in hijabs and strains of Arabic and Turkish all around. Once again, here gathered the displaced and dispossessed. What secrets had they carried on their westward journeys? I wondered. What silences would punctuate the stories they passed on to their children?

It was at Landsberger Allee that Anthony had been asked if he knew how to drive oxen. He answered that he did, even though he had only ever worked with horses, and was hired to work with a pair that lived at a nearby bakery. Once a cart was located, he would be responsible for driving the oxen, though I'm not sure where or for what purpose. In the meantime, the baker asked him to help load bread onto trucks and gave him some to take home each day as payment. Anthony tucked two loaves into his belted coat before returning to the beer hall in the evening. Lucky for my grandfather, the ox cart never materialized, and his husbandry skills were never tested.

After four months in the German capital, Anthony obtained forged documents with false names. Bombs had been falling on the city, and he believed that it would not be long before the Russians arrived. If this happened and he was found, his children would be orphaned, so he set a plan in action.

One by one, he transported the family's bags to the left luggage counter, where baggage could be stored for extended periods, at the train station. Once all was prepared, he took his children, and the four of them disappeared one night without a word. Soon, the war ended, and Lithuania was back under Soviet occupation. Returning home was out of the question, so Anthony set his sights on England.

When my aunt describes the family's time in the postwar displaced person (DP) camps of Braunschweig, Detmold, and Greven, she paints a picture of a simple, austere life led in close quarters (barracks) but not of great hardship. There was food to eat, community to be found, and even schools for my father, still a young boy, to attend. Finally, in 1947, Anthony and his younger daughter left the camp system for good. They made their way to the north of England, where they found work and settled. A year later, the son and elder daughter he'd left behind in Germany joined them in the industrial city of Bradford.

My father rarely talked about his adolescence in that northern English city. I remember only two stories. One was how he used to cover his mouth and nose with his school tie to filter soot from the heavy, polluted air. The other was how England's northerners used to spit out the acronym "DP" like a dirty epithet. Life in that town was, as Bradfordians say, "a mean old scene."

I do not know if Anthony was aware of the evidence the Soviets were gathering against him, but he believed there were spies among Bradford's Lithuanians. Everyone with whom my grandfather shared his suspicions called him paranoid, but it seems he was right. The search file I read in Vilnius shows that the KGB knew exactly where Anthony lived. After keeping a Chicago man by the same name under surveillance, the Soviet secret police realized they had the wrong person and tracked down the right Anthony in England. His home address from that time appears in the file, as do my aunts' and my father's names (though after a single mention, traces of them end). Included are lists of Anthony's correspondents and relatives in America. Apart from the initial confusion with the Chicago man, all the personal information in the document appears to be accurate.

Once called the wool capital of the world, Bradford continues to be known for producing textiles, and perhaps it was the famous Lister's Mill that produced the fabric for Anthony's suit made of "good English wool" that Ona wore in Siberia. In 1947 and 1948, when her children and husband arrived in Bradford, two by two, the factories were still going strong. Anthony and his daughters worked, while my father continued his studies. But soon the regional economy fell into decline. Factories closed and jobs disappeared. The daughters left England for Canada in the 1950s. The son followed in

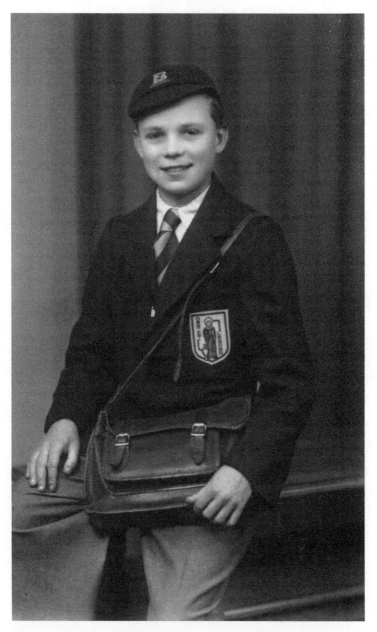

FIG. 20. Ona's son in his English school uniform, circa 1949. Private collection. Courtesy of the author.

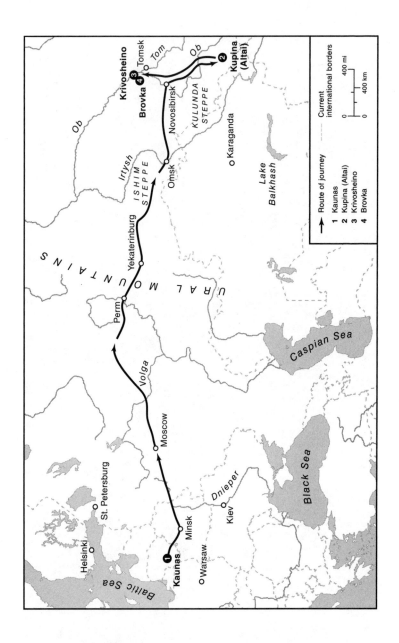

MAP 2. Ona's journey from Kaunas to Brovka, approximately six thousand kilometers. Created by Erin Greb.

1961, after finishing his bachelor's degree at Manchester University. Anthony stayed until 1966, leaving only when he knew Ona had arrived in Canada safely.

Did he ever think of Newtown after that crossing? Would it have been possible to forget?

PART II

Ona

18

A few years after Ona's death in 1996, I began to transcribe the letters she'd written from Siberia to her children. I wanted to know everything about her life there, but I found the letters silenced more than they told. From her Spartan cabin, my grandmother wrote only about the small and mundane; cows, pigs, and gardens were among her favorite subjects. She said almost nothing of the journey by cattle car, of widespread starvation, of taxes paid in agricultural products, or of life under Stalin. This frustrated me, and I felt the creeping pangs of regret. Why had I waited so long to do this? Still, I kept at it. I transcribed in spurts, then packed up the finished product, and sent it to Ona's elder daughter to read over and, if necessary, to correct it. At the very least, I figured it would make a nice gift to my family. The corrected letters returned by courier on the morning I was leaving on a research trip (unrelated to the Siberian letters) to the Kent State University Archives in Ohio.

While tempted to bring the corrections with me, I thought better of it and left the package on my desk at home for fear of misplacing the letters during my trip. Nor could I delay my departure to read them. I'd already postponed my research a week to avoid arriving on the anniversary of the Ohio National Guard's 1970 shootings of student protestors, when the archive would be packed with journalists. I had the rare chance of both the funding and the time for travel, so I had to go and make the most of it.

When I arrived, two boxes of uncataloged papers awaited me. The cartons held unsorted piles of files, seemingly random envelopes full of yellowed clippings, and stacks of handwritten journals. While sifting through one of the boxes, I came across a notebook labeled in Lithuanian, "Father Joseph (1880–1953) in Siberia." A handwritten message clipped to its cover read, in English: "This material was found on a shelf in the Archive, unidentified, on January 2, 1994. It has been placed with these other materials in hope that the next Lithuanian researcher can identify it for us." The seventy-two-page typescript of a taped conversation recorded near Chicago in 1977 told the story of Father Joseph, a priest exiled to Siberia in 1941. The woman interviewed in the transcript, I discovered to my astonishment and even shock, was my grandmother.

A letter, written in a different hand than the one that composed the message asking for help, accompanied the notebook. It was in Lithuanian. My hands shook as I read it:

When Ona came to visit the priest's nephew, a local journalist enthusiastically agreed to interview her and to record the conversation on tape. But when he began the task, it became clear that things were progressing with some difficulty, that he didn't have much time, and what's more it appears that the tape he used produced a very poor recording, and not everything can be understood. Ona told twice as many stories as were recorded. In short, it all ended up a bit of a mess. Later, it was necessary to transcribe the tape, which proved to be a huge job. Not everything could be understood, some parts were skipped over, and so on.

In addition to all that, Ona is a peculiar character. She remained almost completely uneducated, but Siberia hardened her, she became quick-witted and wise. She survived very well and was 73 (at the time of the interview). She rejoined her husband and three children in Canada. I'll send you the text.

Best wishes!
Kazys

The first half of the transcription was mostly intact, but as the pages went on, just as this Kazys's note had warned, the text grew increasingly fragmentary, with ellipses riddling the conversation where the typist ostensibly hadn't been able to make out the recording.

Still, I marveled at how the Chicago interview found its way into Kent's archives, where it then was misshelved. After languishing for almost a decade, the interview was found by one of the few researchers who would recognize its significance. Weirdest of all, that person happened to be the subject's granddaughter. I felt as though an ineffable causality—call it the ghost of my grandmother—had guided me there. I took the notebook in my hands and said, "Okay, I get it. I'll write your book."

How likely was it for such a convergence to occur? What were the odds of my coming across Ona's interview like this, by accident? Even if, on some level, I knew these questions were impossible to answer, I decided to ask them anyway. At the university where I work, a good-natured statistician named Larry agreed to take a shot at my query. "Brace yourself," I wrote, and then I told him the story of finding the interview transcript.

Not surprisingly, Larry could offer no odds. "I do not think it is possible to arrive at any sort of reasonable mathematical calculation of this," he wrote back. Still, his answer turned out to be helpful in unanticipated ways:

It certainly seems to be an amazingly unlikely sequence of events. However, life is full of events and, just by chance, some very unlikely things happen. Think about it this way: A "1-in-one-billion chance" is infinitesimally small. However, if there are 7 billion people on earth, then on average such an event would happen to 7 of them.

Suppose I flew to New York City and went into a library archive, started flipping through documents, and found something about my paternal grandmother that had been misfiled. That seems so unlikely that I cannot imagine it could possibly happen. For one thing, my paternal grandmother was a housewife who lived a quiet life in Pilot Grove, Missouri. I cannot imagine that anyone would have written anything about her let alone something that might be archived. It would be even less likely to be misfiled.

Now your situation is different. Your interest in Lithuanian history is probably, at least in part, due to your ancestry. That part is not completely random. You were looking at an archive at Kent State where . . . information about Lithuanians is stored, which makes it more likely that something about your grandmother might be there. You were specifically looking for information about someone [the Holocaust rescuer Ona Šimaitė] whose name was similar to your grandmother's. Thus the fact a document about her might be misfiled in such a way that you might accidentally find it is more likely. What happened is certainly more likely to have happened to you than to me (or a random person).

The email helped me see that events I had been thinking of as entirely random—first, my grandmother's arrest and deportation and, second, my finding a record of an interview with her about those experiences—were perhaps not so random after all. Larry, in his statistician's vocabulary, had described the stance that allows writers to notice points of overlap in the world. But despite being able to whittle what's random away from what's not, even the statistician appeared to be impressed by my find.

In fact, these eerie coincidences happen with a weird regularity. In *The Red Notebook*, Paul Auster strings together a series of strange and unlikely convergences. I trembled with wonder and recognition as I read his tales of travelers showing up at exactly the right moment, of phone calls from supposedly fictional characters, of siblings unknowingly marrying one another, and of a birth father's being found on what is simultaneously his birthday and the eve of his death. Were these occurrences miracles? Were they caused by something otherworldly? Could a writer really make these things happen simply by living? Or (as Larry would have it) was there a more pedestrian explanation that had to do with ways of seeing and being? Still, even now, I can't shake this coincidence. Or rather, I can't stop it from shaking me.

In *Everything That Rises*, Lawrence Weschler too describes "being visited by similarly uncanny moments of convergence, bizarre associations, eerie rhymes, whispered recollections." It's not by chance, I think, that coincidence came into Weschler's life precisely as he committed himself more fully to his writing. That was the moment he started moving through and seeing the world differently, opening himself up to it in new ways. Writers don't create coincidence. They notice it.

But even Weschler couldn't resist wondering if there wasn't actually something more powerful, divine even, at work. While visiting Donald Judd's mammoth sculptural installation absurdly situated in the Texan desert, the author watches an insect move a straw across the earth. The ant nudges and adjusts the straw, then pulls back to appraise its work. Satisfied, the creature turns around and leaves its own (relatively speaking) mammoth installation behind, also absurdly situated in the Texan desert. What to make of such an occurrence? Weschler wonders: "Had Judd first got [the notion for his installation] from the ant, or the ant from the [sculptures], or was it that Judd had conditioned me even to be able to notice the ant, or was the ant simply God (or, at the very least, God's high priest), or *what*?"

Perhaps my work has conditioned me to notice things like the notebook. And perhaps a series of unlikely though not entirely random events put that notebook into my hands. But maybe, just as Weschler wondered as he watched the ant-sculptor, something divine was at work that day in the archive. What I didn't realize was that to write Ona's book would mean writing Anthony's as well. And that between those two lives I would find another eerie kind of fate in which the one paid for the crimes of the other—even before they had been committed.

19

June 1941.

The Kaunas station teemed. Ona stood against a wall with a suitcase at her feet. She looked around, hoping to spot Anthony but also praying he wouldn't be there. He was nowhere to be seen. Women and children abounded. They carried bags and linen bundles. A little girl watched in terror as soldiers dragged a husband from his wife.

Guards loaded everyone onto a passenger train, where they stayed for perhaps an hour, maybe two. Ona wouldn't be able to say with certainty how long when the interviewer asked the question many years later. Next came roll call. She responded to her own name and recognized no others until she heard the soldier holler for a "Father Joseph." An elderly man answered and raised his hand but remained seated on his suitcase. He was impressive in his dignity and calm. Squeezing past a nursing mother and whimpering child, Ona made her way over to him.

"Excuse me," she said quietly, "but aren't you from the village of P——?" The man looked up, startled at the mention of his hometown.

"I'm from the same region," Ona told him. "Do you have a brother? I think my mother was his Catholic confirmation sponsor."

"We're family!" The priest extended his hand.

Father Joseph hailed from one of the wealthiest families in

Lithuania. As rumors of coming deportations began to circulate, the priest's twin brother sensed he was in danger and fled to the West. Father Joseph, by contrast, refused to budge. Instead, he'd packed his bags and waited for Red Army soldiers to arrive and arrest him.

As Ona and the priest talked, a string of cattle cars rumbled up a parallel track. This, not the passenger train, would take them east.

Among bits of straw and traces of manure, Ona and Father Joseph staked out an area in one corner on the car's wooden floor. Teenagers clambered atop shelves and set up camp by the small windows above. Soon the wheels began to turn.

The car moved slowly past a prison camp with barbed-wire fences, through the church-spired capital and its new suburbs, into unfamiliar Belarus and finally Russia.

"Where are they taking us?" Ona whispered to the priest leaning against the wall beside her. She knew the answer, though, before he'd uttered it.

"Siberia."

For four days and nights, the priest and Ona slept fitfully. Each rolled over only when the other did, since they were not only huddled against each other but also squeezed between the car's wall and a mother with her three children.

As the exiles rumbled eastward, birch stands and pine forests gave way to wetlands and then to a rolling landscape dotted with scrubby brush. They passed villagers tending gardens of cabbages, beans, and potatoes. Convoys stacked with logs trundled by on a neighboring track, testifying to mighty forests somewhere close.

Soon children grew hungry and began to cry. Some deportees, including Father Joseph, had thought to bring food. Though he shared what he had, the priest warned his fellow travelers to ration carefully.

Days passed, and with each sunrise, mothers assured their children that today there would be food, but as the hours slipped by and their bellies ached, the mothers' promises showed themselves to be hollow. The children drifted off into fitful sleep. With each kilometer, the air in the car grew closer. A nearby woman became hysterical. Ona sat. She neither screamed nor slept.

On the fifth day of travel, far from home, the cattle car's door opened with a thud to reveal a soup cauldron some yards from the tracks. The priest, who spoke fluent Russian from his St. Petersburg student days, translated the guards' instructions.

"They're letting one parent from each family off. You must leave your children on the train. Bring a cup," he said, loud enough for all to hear.

Childless adults, who had every reason to attempt an escape, had to stay put. Ona remained on the train.

Soon, all around, famished children gulped watery soup from cups, jars, and bottles. Ona felt no hunger. In the faces of the kids around her, she saw those of her own, and in their voices she heard her babies' cries. When she closed her eyes, she saw her daughters' and son's legs carrying them down the tracks as they called after her train. Father Joseph whispered prayer after prayer beside her. In time, she began to whisper too.

In Ona's train car, women organized to maintain as much dignity as they could and hung sheets around a hole cut in the car's floor, so the exiles could relieve themselves in relative privacy. The sheets are a detail that appears in virtually every deportation memoir.

Survivors also have told of bodies strewn alongside the railway. The dead, they say, were tossed out of the cars to make room for the living. Mothers, in particular, went crazy when forced to leave the body of a dead child behind. Ona, however, told nothing of such scenes—neither to us, her family, nor to the interviewer who recorded a lengthy conversation with her many years after her return. Perhaps she couldn't see out to the ground from the corner she shared with the priest? Perhaps her cohort was luckier or stronger and fared better? Or maybe these were details she chose not to recall.

20

The Soviet regime did not invent Siberian deportation. As early as the late seventeenth century, banishment to regions beyond the Ural Mountains had largely replaced the death penalty in Russia. Rather than beheading or drawing and quartering mutineers, murderers, and thieves, authorities exiled them instead. They marked the banished with slit nostrils, severed ears, brands, and tattoos so that, even if they escaped Siberia, they could never evade identification and humiliation. Eventually, punishment through exile targeted POWs, counterfeiters, military deserters, aging and infirm serfs, loan defaulters, and Old Believers deemed heretical for their rejection of post-reform Russian Orthodox dogma.

Throughout the seventeenth, eighteenth, and nineteenth centuries, Siberian marches took up to two years to complete. Convoys of prisoners shackled in iron walked up to five thousand kilometers eastward through snow, marshland, and insect swarms. In 1863 barges came into use to transport exiles for part of their journey, but first they had to make it to the north-flowing river system on foot.

Exile had a purpose besides simple punishment: Russia's unwanted, destitute, and criminal elements were to settle the vast open land and conquer its native peoples—the reindeer herders, hunter-gatherers, fishers, and nomads—who had lived there for millennia. Officials hoped that a lasting, more recognizably Russian society would ultimately take root and grow on the steppes and tundra. But for this to happen, they soon realized that families—specifically, women—were needed.

Hoping to engineer family units, the Russian government attempted to procure wives for exiles. They offered to buy indigenous Siberian girls at a price of 150 rubles per head. It didn't work. Indigenous families refused to sell their daughters, though Siberia's male peasants gave up their female relatives to exiles for 50 rubles each. But despite these and other incentives—tax breaks for first marriages and cash rewards for successful matches—by 1828, Siberian settlements still failed to thrive and for the same reason: a lack of women.

Unlike Ona, who traveled over the Urals without her family, most women who ended up in Siberia in the nineteenth century were wives accompanying husbands into exile. Often these women marched with their spouses by choice, since being left behind as a convict's widow could be a much harder fate than a life in exile, so strong was the stigma of Siberian punishment. In other cases, women ended up there because of crimes they had committed, though few—around 20 percent—had been convicted for serious offenses. The journey for female exiles was far more perilous than for men making the same trip. When stopping for shelter in fetid stations along the way, both women and children risked sexual attack.

The region's long-standing gender disparity, with men massively outnumbering women, changed dramatically under Stalin. The special settlements of the 1930s through the 1950s were overwhelmingly female, since most of the wives of the so-called enemies of the people (like Ona) ended up there. Although life was very difficult on the settlements, it was still a far cry from the Gulag, and female exiles had much better chances for survival. By 1941, the year the USSR officially entered World War II, the ratio of women to men in some rural areas of the Soviet Union had widened to 6:1. Staggering Soviet military losses in World War II would only heighten the disproportion.

Ona's closest male confidant in Siberia was the elderly priest who traveled with her into exile. In contrast to my grandmother's seventeen years, his banishment was comparatively short. Father Joseph was allowed to return to Lithuania after only four winters, when the chairman of the Presidium of the Supreme Soviet of the Lithuanian SSR intervened on his behalf. Why the chairman did so is unclear. Some say he was repaying an old favor; others are more cynical and believe the priest's release was calculated. Indeed, archived documents confirm that upon Father Joseph's return to Kaunas in 1944, authorities tried to recruit him as an informant for the KGB. When they failed, the secret police planned to exile the priest once again in 1953. Father Joseph died before it could happen.

21

For two weeks, the exiles' train rolled past shabby settlements and across scrubland until it crossed the Ural Mountains, the gateway to Siberia. From their second-story perches, the teenagers marveled at the trains bursting with soldiers and munitions that moved past them as their locomotive stopped to give way. They helped Father Joseph up to a window so he could ask a passing Russian worker what was happening. *Voina* (war) was the answer.

Nazi Germany had invaded the Soviet Union and, with it, Lithuania. The Luftwaffe had bombed the latter's capital, Vilnius, and the Wehrmacht had taken the country. From deep inside the car's throng, a woman shouted for joy at the news.

"We're saved," said Ona, helping the priest set his feet back down on the car's floor. "The army will need every train, and they'll dump us out on the tundra. We'll walk home."

But the train didn't stop. It pushed farther and farther east and then suddenly dipped south, until it finally came to a halt.

The high window framed the windblown steppes of the Altai, a region suffering through a third consecutive year of drought. Livestock milled in the distance. Skinny as fence posts, what looked to be goats revealed themselves, upon closer inspection, to be malnourished cows. With no timber to burn, the people who lived off this land made fuel by mixing together manure and straw and tamping them down.

The village of Kupina was a collection of mud huts located a little over halfway between Kaunas and Tomsk. It was peopled with Ukrainians exiled to one of thousands of special settlements starting in 1932, when Stalin deported three hundred thousand people from Ukraine to Siberia and then systematically starved the millions left behind to death.

Authorities moved exiles around Siberia, from settlement to settlement, depending on what work was to be done and on the whims of the regime. Some deportees speculated that these transfers were intended to heighten their sense of insecurity. Those taken to the Far North, near the Arctic Circle, landed on wild terrain without shelter or building materials. Though it was still midsummer, cold winds blew. New arrivals huddled under upturned boats and inside tents made of American flour sacks while they waited for lumber to arrive. Farther south along the shore, others built makeshift barracks of logs pulled from rivers. They sealed the gaps between them with mud, fashioned bricks for clay ovens by hand, and improvised thatched roofs by laying birch bark on manure. Where there were hills, exiles burrowed and created turf houses.

On the steppes of Kupina, Ona exited the train for the first time since boarding in Lithuania. When her feet hit the ground, though, she could barely stand. The earth moved under her, surging forward with an irresistible force.

"Train legs," the priest laughed, watching her stumble.

All around them stretched wide, brown, and treeless plains. No guns pointed at them here. No violence threatened. No guards glowered. But there was no escape, only wind and emptiness.

Exhausted deportees collapsed onto the floor of Kupina's schoolhouse, the sole wooden building in the village. They bedded down on top of whatever bundles they had brought with them. In the morning, seasoned and strong Ukrainian women roused the ragged travelers. They brought milk, onions, and fresh cheese for the newcomers. It was a staggering gesture of generosity, given how little these people had themselves. Doubtless they remembered their own journeys into this land, when they too had been forced onto trains a half decade earlier. "Kindness all around," Ona would say, remembering those women.

22

For twelve days, the exiles stayed on the steppes and helped harvest the spindly wheat crop. Once the work was complete, Ona and her fellow exiles were herded onto trucks and traveled back to the train once again. They continued by rail for another two days, stopping at the docks of Novosibirsk just before dawn.

In the time they had spent in the Altai, Ona and her companions had learned of a factory that made Siberian felt boots. Everyone who could had bought a pair. Ultimately, the boots protected Ona's toes, health, and possibly her life. She put them on at the first sign of Siberian winter and didn't take them off for six months. As thick as her index finger was long, the boots came up to her knees. "It was like walking with stumps," she laughed, remembering them decades later. Besides bread and milk, the boots were the last things she would buy for many years.

At the docks of Novosibirsk, the train jogged back and forth for what seemed an eternity. Clutching their new boots, deportees shuffled and banged against one another. Finally, the convoy slunk onto a series of three connected barges, and when they emerged from the train, the exiles caught sight of a Siberian river for the first time—the massive Ob.

Rivers were key not only to the exile system but also to Siberia's economy, culture, and climate. In summer, barges moved goods and people. All winter, even today, the frozen waterways served as ice roads for transport trucks. Those who have never visited Siberia often imagine the region to be a solid expanse of ice and snow, a wasteland in all seasons. But, in truth, the land of eastern Russia is incredibly diverse. Much of it is temperate and blanketed with birch, pine, aspen, and larch trees. Its forests teem with wildlife and mushrooms, its waters with fish, and its fields with berries. Parts of the area, such as the region of Krasnoyarsk—as one daughter of deportees described it to me—are mountainous, lake speckled, and beautiful, especially in spring when wildflowers abound.

But the north-flowing rivers result in an inescapable climactic challenge. In winter, the rivers that feed into Arctic waters freeze first at their mouths. Once this happens, ice clogs the northern flow. And as the water freezes ever farther south, the rivers spill over banks, flooding the land far and wide. The process happens every year, and as a result, much of Siberia is a swamp.

Wetlands breed insects. More than the cold or even the hunger or the hard work, it was the Siberian mosquitoes that tortured Ona in exile. On spring and summer evenings, she tied her cuffs with rags before sitting down to write letters, but even this didn't prevent insects from biting a bracelet-like ring around her hand. The smoke she used to keep them out of the house made it impossible to breathe, but without the smoke, the mosquitoes would have made it impossible to live.

As the exiles traveled up the broad and slow-moving Ob, they roamed the barges. Compared to the cramped conditions of the cattle cars, life on the water was a pleasure. They basked in the sun and breathed in the fresh air while traveling a river so wide they were also free of buzzing pests. They had what they needed to bathe and to drink, and with no work assignments, the exiles could finally relax. As she floated and watched the Ob's shore, Ona listened to the chatter of languages both familiar and strange: Bessarabian, Latvian, Lithuanian, Estonian.

The barges eventually docked where the land was flat and fertile enough to grow vegetables. Ona and her fellow captives first made

FIG. 21. The Ob River, 2010. Photo by the author.

their way to a village in ruins for a couple of nights, and then they were inexplicably sent back to the docks for another two days. There again, with nowhere to run and no escape possible without watercraft, guards were unnecessary. Finally, a couple hundred people were taken to Krivosheino, a Russian village whose locals greeted the exiles with bread. The newcomers built fires and boiled water for the tea they had bought at the village store. After a month of travel and uprootedness, and perhaps despite themselves, the deportees had begun to establish patterns and to configure themselves. They formed family-size groups and pairings like that of Ona and Father Joseph. Another five Lithuanians, women and children, now joined them, and together the seven constituted a unit of makeshift kin.

Only three thousand Lithuanian exiles found themselves in the Tomsk region before 1945, and then another few thousand joined them in the postwar years. Most others ended up in the Altai, Novosibirsk, Kazakhstan, and the Komi region. As for accommodations, Ona was among the fortunate. She and her companions would not live in mud huts or in improvised tents; instead, they would live in an established village.

With the country at war, farm workers were scarce, so deportees cultivated Siberia's land to feed the Soviet Union. Supervisors from various collectives arrived on horseback to choose laborers. They sought strong, capable people. One selected Ona immediately.

"We are seven," she said to the man in the saddle. "If you want me, you must take the others too."

I imagine Ona came into her own in Siberia. Distance and hardship either forced or allowed her to locate a power within herself. The wife of an authoritarian and militaristic man, she must have deferred to her husband for years before her arrest. But in a strange and surprising way, Siberia made her mighty. There, Ona had no choice but to take up "men's work," as she called it in the letters she wrote over the decades that followed. She donned her husband's suit and assumed the role of protector of the weak. The first sign of this newfound strength and courage showed itself that day the workers were sorted and she dared issue an ultimatum to the man who looked her over.

Her demand worked. In August 1941 Ona and her six new kin set out for Brovka's dairy farm together.

23

In 2010 I decided to try and find my grandmother's place of exile. I hoped that in going to Siberia, the place would change in my imagination. Perhaps instead of thinking of Siberia only as a wound and a source of family trauma, I could come to see it as a real place of living people. I figured there had to be more to Siberia than Gulags and graveyards. After all, it was also home to ancient nomadic cultures of reindeer herders, lost colonies of heretical Russian Old Believers, solitary grizzly bears, majestic mountains, and modern cities. So, in preparation for my journey, I began to read and dream. Soon, instead of fear, I started to feel anticipation.

Though I initially had no idea where on the vast map of Siberia to find Ona's village, after enlisting the help of a Russian friend, Elena, Brovka turned out to be quite easy to locate. Native knowledge goes a long way, and within minutes, Elena had made her way to the home page of Krivosheino District (a place-name I'd pulled from one of Ona's letters), where she found a map. A detail from the website showed a river called Brovka. Along its shore lay a village named, in turn, Upper Brovka (there was no Lower Brovka), situated only three kilometers from a place called Bielastok (or Belostok). A memory of something I once read in Ona's letters returned to me; Bielastok—named for Białystok, the city of origin of the migrants who established the settlement—had to be the village that my grandmother described as a Polish kolkhoz.

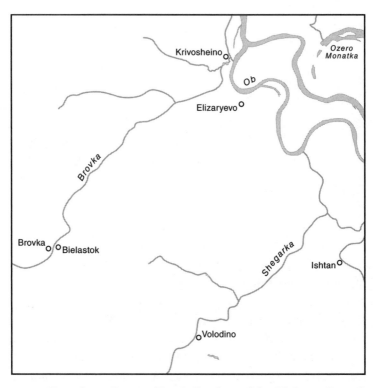

MAP 3. Krivosheino District, Tomsk, Brovka, and the Ob River. Created by Erin Greb.

I sat down on the floor to study the maps I'd printed. One put Siberia squarely at its center, so that Lithuania lay sideways, its small territory slinking down the earth's curvature. Snaking my fingers up from the city of Tomsk, I followed the River Ob northward until I found Krivosheino and, by extension, nearby Brovka.

Of my entire family, my cousin Darius was the only one who didn't tell me I was crazy for wanting to visit Ona's village. Other relatives voiced worries about food, safety, the harsh climate, and recent environmental (nuclear) disasters. Again and again, I heard, "You can't go *there*!" Finally, with tickets booked and contacts made, I showed that I could. Only once Darius had agreed to travel with me, though, did everyone else breathe a sigh of relief.

The summer of our trip to Siberia was Russia's hottest on record, with temperatures reaching the high thirties and low forties Celsius. Forest fires burned throughout the country, but the blazes that the Russian government lamented as a "natural disaster" were nothing of the sort. They had resulted from a systematic mismanagement of the land. Wetlands were drained and mined for peat, huge territories had been handed over to private corporations, and the country's forest ministry was reduced to a skeleton staff of twelve individuals who were so swamped with paperwork they could not patrol the lands for which they were responsible. But now, the mismanagement of the countryside had begun to affect city dwellers.

When we landed in Moscow in early August, the streets outside the airport were suffocating. Smoke and smog hung heavily in the air and weighed in our lungs. Health authorities cautioned citizens to remain indoors, to air-condition their apartments, and to stay off the streets. Despite the warnings, Moscow's roads teemed with cars that spewed ever more fumes into the atmosphere. The death rate rose dramatically, and the city's top doctor reported seven hundred mortalities per day.

That evening, my cousin and I boarded the eastbound train that would be our home for four days. Already exhausted from our journey to that point, we slept deeply until morning and awoke to the sight of the birch stands and pine forests while we went rushing past. I sat in my bedclothes for hours, watching as the rolling landscape gave way to swampland and back. Darius, who lives among the redwoods of northern California, marveled at the scrawny trees. The scent of smoke still seeped into our cabin through its sealed windows.

My cousin and I had each brought copious amounts of reading material, anticipating boredom and long yawning stretches as we traveled across Russia. This was not the case. Instead, our time passed easily, and I found myself gripped by my cousin's stories about the grandmother he had known so much better than I. As he remembered her to me, Darius described how Ona had felt to the touch, how she'd moved, and how easily she'd laughed.

That night, after our first full day of train travel, I lay on my berth, listening to the wheels rumbling against the rails. I calculated that when my grandmother had made this very trip by cattle car, Ona had been thirty-six, a year younger than I was that summer.

Would I have survived a similar fate?

On train platforms along the way, we observed elderly women selling flowers and berries by the cupful. Vendors offered beer and little homemade meals of boiled potatoes and chicken, holding their wares up to the train's windows for inspection as it slowed to a stop.

Eventually, Darius and I decided to take advantage of the platform commerce. We waited to get off the train in hope of finding some ice cream to buy. Our *provodnitsa*, the Russian "train hostess" who kept an eye on all the goings-on in the car, joined us and stood at the ready with her key. Despite my guidebook's warnings about these train women and how one must never cross them, our *provodnitsa* had a sweet disposition. She liked order and took her job very seriously, locking our cabin door whenever we left our quarters and offering to bring us mineral water to drink. She vacuumed daily and was constantly bending over to tidy the long, thin piece of linen that covered the corridor carpets. It was a sort of long dish towel that kept the actual rug from getting stepped on—a redundancy that struck me as both crazy and charming.

As the train rumbled to a stop, I noticed the *provodnitsa* had changed out of her uniform and into a roomy flowery dress, so I asked if her day was over. No, she answered, she was going all the way home to Tomsk. Then she inquired about us.

"Us too," I replied. "We're headed to a place near Tomsk where our grandmother lived for seventeen years—Brovka, near the Ob."

Though I hadn't used the word "exile," the *provodnitsa*'s face fell, and she became uncomfortable, as if I'd told her that we were going to visit the site of a family member's murder. Then she said something about her own family (her mother, perhaps?) who had also been deported or imprisoned. I understood the word *lager* (camp), but I had a hard time following her with my meager Russian skills.

I didn't know what else to say. She opened the door, and we nodded to one another in silence.

24

Brovka's sister village, Bielastok, was the older of the two neighboring settlements. After moving to the marshy and buggy Tomsk region of Siberia voluntarily, a small group of Poles had put down stakes and named their new town after their home city of Białystok, which was part of the Russian Empire during the nineteenth-century Siberian migration. The Białystokers came east to populate the territory the czar had granted, building homes, a Polish-language school, and even a Catholic church named for Saint Anthony of Padua, patron saint of lost things—perhaps even of lost homelands and families. The Poles planted gardens, raised animals, and managed to survive on those harsh acres.

In 1937 during Stalin's Great Terror, Bielastok's Saint Anthony's Church was closed. Thieves took its organ and furniture and destroyed its icons. Reopened on the saint's feast day in June 1998, the sanctuary is now the last wooden Catholic church in western Siberia and one of only two in the entire Tomsk region. A Polish priest from the homeland celebrates Mass every Sunday. Cultural differences between Polish Poles and Siberian Poles have proven to be great, and during our days in the village Darius and I heard stories of tensions between the cleric and his parishioners.

"I don't understand a thing that priest says," ranted one elderly Bielastoker, complaining of the cleric's accent and general foreignness. "I told him, *I built that church*! Now, *you* go pray."

FIG. 22. Saint Anthony's Church, 2010. Photo by the author.

Only around 1920, several decades after the Poles had settled, did Belarusians arrive, fleeing famine and typhus. These arrivals were even poorer and more ragged than the Polish villagers of Bielastok, who called the newcomers "shlep-shoes," in imitation of the sound their birch-bark footwear made when they walked. The Belarusians built their own village, right across the river from

Bielastok, and called their new home Brovka after the waterway that separated them from their neighbors. By all accounts, Polish Bielastokers did not receive the Belarusian Brovkans with open arms, resenting these shabby Slavic cousins for sponging off their decades-long work to render the marshland of the Tomsk region arable. Conflicts arose. Children tousled in fistfights and hurled insults at one another across the river.

Over the days we spent in Bielastok-Brovka, Darius and I pieced together the origin story of these two villages. As a result, we finally began to make sense of a part of Ona's tale that we'd never really understood. She'd always told us that she'd felt more accepted by the Orthodox Belarusians (in Brovka) than by the Catholic Poles (in Bielastok), although, culturally speaking, she should have had more in common with the latter. I now suspect that the Polish villagers of Bielastok may have been less than welcoming to the forced Lithuanian exiles because, just as the Belarusians had arrived to the relatively cushy environment that the Poles had created, here now they had to accommodate a trainload of other deportees. Ona's perceived rejection wasn't personal; it was likely simply a manifestation of local culture and of the universal suspicion and resentment of old-timers toward newcomers.

The Polish and Belarusian communities lived side by side until the last house in Brovka was demolished in 1990. Any past animosities seem to have dissipated, because when I asked what had happened to Brovka's last inhabitants, my guide shrugged and replied that they had moved to Bielastok. Even their languages eventually melded. Today's Bielastokers speak a version of the Polish language that has become so infused with Belarusian and Siberian Russian that twenty-first-century linguists travel there to study the isolated community.

Though Ona traveled there by barge, Darius and I made our way to her place of exile by car. From Tomsk, our trip to Brovka and Bielastok on a surprisingly modern highway took around two hours. Off in the distance, the Ob River looked nothing like our Canadian waterways. There were no large rocks, no brush on its banks. Men fished along its edge, and I wondered about the water's toxicity. Fallout from a nuclear accident almost two decades earlier had been the main argument my husband had used to try and sway me from making the Siberian trip.

Several months after I returned from Siberia, I read a scientific article describing contamination levels in the Ob. Much of the analysis eluded me, but I learned that its water and silt contain alarming levels of radioactive isotopes (plutonium and neptunium) from pre-1963 nuclear arms testing and from later underground tests conducted at weapons plants located on the river's tributaries. Arms production had begun in the region in 1949 (when Ona lived there), and the study described precariously stored nuclear waste in the area. The crisis came in 1993 when a waste tank exploded at the then secret installation called Tomsk-7.

As we approached the Ob, I could make out Tomsk-7's cooling towers in the distance. When I asked about the accident, our driver laughed, telling me it had been no big deal, "just a radioactive cloud." My husband later commented that this levity was probably a survival strategy. After all, what choice did Tomsk residents have but to be cavalier?

At the sign for Bielastok, we took a sharp left turn, then bumped down a winding road and past a pond that the locals jokingly called Lake Baikal. The setting sun outlined the silhouettes of two shirtless boys headed for a dip. With its blue-shuttered houses and blue fences, its kitchen gardens and carved ornamentation, Bielastok looked similar to the villages we'd passed while on the train. Aging neighbors smiled toothlessly and looked us over as they sat and chatted over tea and cigarettes, watching the day disappear over the horizon. Apart from gaining electricity and natural gas lines for heat, I imagine little has changed in these villagers' way of life since the 1950s.

But today, Bielastok is dying. This is undeniable. Already in 2010, at the time of our visit, it was a village of old women, widows for

FIG. 23. Bielastok, 2010. Photo by the author.

the most part. The youth are leaving, especially the young men. It's no longer possible to live or raise a family on the wages paid at the farm, I was told, so everyone moves on.

Buses used to run here three times a day, but service recently dwindled to three times a week. Children are present in significant numbers only during summer holidays, when they come from Tomsk to visit their grandparents. The kids we met glowed with happiness and curiosity. Darius and I watched in amazement as five-year-old Vanya rode up and down the village's main drag on a giant horse at least four times his height. (Inevitably, late in the day, the horse spooked, and the boy fell.) When their grandparents die, will these children have any reason to come to Bielastok? At the time of our visit, only forty-two children were registered at the local school, and its administration had to lobby hard to keep it open, arguing for the benefits of its distinct cultural and linguistic education. The next day, when we went from house to house, making inquiries, I found myself wondering if we were meeting the village's last inhabitants.

Never did Ona believe she would spend close to two decades in Siberia. Three years in Brovka, tops, she figured, despite the twenty-year service contract she'd been required to sign upon her arrival at the collective farm in 1941. When the war ended, she reasoned, she would be able to go home.

Brovka's exiles followed the war as closely as they could. Their tools: a propagandistic regional newspaper and an atlas borrowed from the village schoolchildren. As they tracked the front, Ona and her fellow Lithuanians rejoiced at each German advance, believing every Soviet loss moved them closer to salvation. Not one of them could imagine the ghettos and mass graves that now mired their homeland. None envisioned the bullet-riddled forests or that their loved ones might be involved in the slaughter. Only Father Joseph warned against celebration, predicting Germany's defeat.

"Once the Americans join the Russians," he said gravely, "we'll all be buried alive."

He wasn't wrong. The Red Army reoccupied Lithuania in 1944, at which point a new wave of Siberian deportations began. It ended only in 1953, the year of Stalin's death. Over nine years, 111,000 more Lithuanians were sent into exile. Although far larger in scale, these later deportations targeted more select groups than those of 1941. For example, 1947 saw the mass deportation of Lithuanian so-called kulaks, or wealthy peasants. Also targeted were families suspected of or found to be supporting the Forest Brothers—guerrilla fighters who, from 1944, waged an armed resistance against Soviet occupation. But in 1941 Soviet victory had seemed impossible to both the exiles and the local Siberians.

Even the village boys drafted into the Red Army were rooting for the Germans. They vowed not to shoot the enemy and promised to surrender as prisoners of war instead. Deeply embedded in this culture was the image of Germans as hardworking, honest, and cultured. In 1762, Catherine the Great invited ethnic Germans to settle along the Volga River. German-speaking Lutherans, Catholics, and Mennonites arrived in the eighteenth century to enjoy land grants, tax breaks, military service exemptions, and religious freedoms offered by the Russian monarch. They came to be called Volga Germans and lived peacefully alongside Russians for centuries.

But the Siberians who went to fight (or, rather, to surrender) soon discovered that the Germans of the Third Reich were not at all like those in Russia. Young men began to return with stories from the front. They told of how they had been held and starved in pens so crowded that only the deceased could lie down. By the end of 1941, two-thirds of the three million Soviet soldiers taken prisoner by Germany were dead. According to the historian Timothy Snyder, "As many Soviet prisoners of war died *on a single given day* in autumn 1941 as did British and American prisoners of war over the course of the entire Second World War."

Back in German-occupied Lithuania, 11,500 Soviet prisoners of war had ended up in Newtown, where Anthony was working as police chief. They had been marched there from the front lines, and judging from the photographs that Romas showed me when we met in Lithuania, most had been Central Asians. Some may even have come from places not too far from Brovka and Bielastok. The Germans designed their Soviet POW camps to end life. No one in the Nazi administration disputed the fact that these holding pens were, in fact, passive killing machines. Indeed, Alfred Rosenberg once said, "The more of these prisoners die, the better for us." Captives were counted but not registered by name. Authorities made no provisions for food, shelter, or medical care. There were no clinics, toilets, or other sanitation facilities. Shelter from the elements was scarce. Daily calorie quotients fell far below survival levels.

All this was true of Newtown's POW camp. Everything we know about that city's Oflag 60 comes from German and Soviet postwar investigations. No official camp documents survived the war. There are no extant prisoner memoirs or diaries. Oflag 60, though an officers' camp by name (Oflag stands for *Offizierlager*), actually functioned as a Stalag (*Stammlager*), or camp for rank-and-file prisoners. In operation from the summer of 1941 until the summer of 1942, Oflag 60 was overcrowded from the beginning. Prisoners lived in makeshift sheds that they themselves built upon arrival.

FIG. 24. Prisoners of Oflag 60, 1941. Private collection. Courtesy of
Romas Treideris.

Though the vast majority of Newtown's POWs died of starvation,
typhus, and exhaustion, they faced active violence too. Each week,
the camp's commando and sometimes its guards selected and executed certain prisoners. I imagine this practice was the captors' way
of terrorizing and therefore exerting control over the rest. Every
one of those anonymous prisoners now lies buried in a mass grave
in Newtown's Jewish cemetery, alongside the victims of the city's
first two massacres—the killings of Lithuanian communists and
of Jewish men.

To make matters worse for the Soviet POWs, Stalin was suspicious
and unforgiving of those who did not resist and were taken captive.
His Order 227, issued in July 1942 and known as "Not a Step Back,"
declared: "Panic-mongers and cowards are to be exterminated on
sight." When Soviet POWs were finally released in 1945, the tyrant
sent penal brigades to hunt them down, calling them "a dangerous,
fainthearted, cowardly element." After surviving the Nazi prison
camps, many young soldiers were then sent to Siberia for up to
twenty-five years.

25

Over the first three years of exile, Ona's life comprised a thousand tiny details of survival. She and her six companions lived in a single room and slept on narrow wooden cots. One sleeper could turn over only when all of them did. They pooled their resources and ate together. When time allowed, they told stories by the stove in the evenings. By day they went out to work.

The exiles toiled on the farm or in the forest. Tree felling—a job that most village women, including Ona, did in the early days of the war—was the most dangerous of assignments. During the war years, Soviet aircraft factories needed wood, so the collective farm sent teenage girls and adult women to harvest straight trees of specified lengths. They had no training and learned as they went. Timber often fell without warning, killing workers below. When I visited the village in 2010, an elderly Bielastoker named Anna told me how, when she was out cutting trees as a girl, a massive trunk had come down unexpectedly. It had grazed her nose as it fell, she said, brushing her fingers across her face for emphasis. When it landed with a crash on the toes of her boots, luckily, they were several sizes too big, and the tree crushed only leather and air. Anna's face lit up in a one-toothed laugh at this detail.

We talked in her immaculate house. A carpet hung on a wall beside her, and a wind-up alarm clock ticked loudly on the table. Anna wore

FIG. 25. Anna with the church key, 2010. Photo by the author.

a pink T-shirt with the words "Black Rose" emblazoned in English across her chest. She'd paired it with a tidy navy blue skirt and requisite floral headscarf. In the photograph I took at the end of our meeting, Anna displays the village key to Saint Anthony's Church.

"Your grandmother was very religious," she said. "Very spiritual. She used to tell the workers at the farm that the only way to survive was to maintain faith. That if you believed in God, everything would be all right."

For some deportees, the experience of being ripped from their homes and separated from their families shook their faith. But for others, religious practice became a symbol of resistance. In the absence of men, and especially of male clergy (for whom it was dangerous to minister openly), women formed their own prayer circles. Now, for the first time, I understood that maintaining her belief in God had been a revolutionary act on Ona's part. Whereas in every other way, she seems to have put her head down, carried out her work diligently, and kept her opinions to herself, in this small way, she revolted. She continued to talk to God.

In addition to tree felling, Brovka's women were also assigned to wintertime threshing. Since Siberia's growing season lasts only a few short months, it was all the workers of the collective farm could do to harvest their grain by the end of summer. They left threshing for the winter. Although combine harvesters eventually came to Brovka, in wartime it was humans, not horses, that powered the threshers.

First, the workers split the straw from the grain, a process that took all day. Then they spent the night separating wheat from chaff. This job took three people: one worker poured the grain; a second walked round and round, turning the machine; and a third collected the separated kernels. The work was done far from the village, and Ona often arrived at the thresher to find the wheat frozen and covered in snow. To keep warm, they burned mountains of straw and burrowed into piles of insulating chaff during breaks.

Eventually, conditions improved. Within three years of their arrival, Ona and her fellow Brovkans turned to tending animals. Each worker specialized in one aspect of dairy farming. Ona's specialty was tending calves, a comparatively good lot for a deportee. Whereas some exiles froze their hands cleaning fish in the Arctic or choked on deadly dust in mines, Ona spent cold days among the warm bodies and soft eyes of young creatures. She gave each of them a name that they learned to recognize. In spring, when she called, her calves would come barreling from the fields to greet her. In winter, they flanked her in the barn, nuzzling up against her thighs and exhaling long streams of vapor.

Nina, one of the farm's milkers, had lived for a time in Ona's house as a young woman. Darius and I sat at her kitchen table, listening as she talked. Nina's gray hair was plaited and pulled into a low bun. Like Anna, she too was in her eighties. Out through the window, I could see haystacks and a mustard-yellow Lada. Nina's family's home had been far away, she explained, thus she'd had to set out for work in the middle of the night. Since Ona had lived

FIG. 26. Ona tending animals in Siberia, 1949. Private collection. Courtesy of the author.

very close to their workplace, she'd offered the girl a place to sleep. Nina couldn't remember hearing much about Ona's children, but when I asked her about Agnieszka, my grandmother's cow, she laughed and nodded. "Yes, she was black and white."

I pulled out a few photographs, trying to jog more memories. Nina apologized for her poor eyesight as she flipped through the pictures, predicting she would be of little help, but after an instant, she paused at an image saying, "This one looks familiar." It showed Ona sitting by her Siberian house. A few minutes later, we understood why she had recognized the image.

Above my head in the kitchen hung a picture frame filled with black-and-white photographs. We'd seen similar collages in each house we'd visited. Often these frames hung well above eye level and were decorated with white paper doilies. Giving Nina some space to look at the photos without pressure, or perhaps just trying to take everything in, I glanced up at a frame above my head. Toward its bottom, I found a copy of the very same photograph of my grandmother that Nina had recognized. With yelps of surprise and excitement, Darius and I jumped up to examine all the frames in the house carefully, looking for more traces of our grandmother. It wasn't long before we'd found one in the next room—a group snapshot taken in Canada in 1957. It showed all of Ona's children, their spouses, and her first grandchild.

More convergences.

26

Between 1946 and 1948, close to two million people died in the Soviet Union as a direct result of starvation and malnutrition. But city dwellers perished in far greater numbers than did those in villages like Brovka and Bielastok, where both exiles and migrants shared wisdom and natural resources to survive. Some deportees carried knowledge of edible and medicinal plants with them into Siberia. They prepared dishes made from tree bark to supplement their diets during the years of famine.

In Ona's case, Brovka's long-standing villagers taught her to forage and showed her which wild plants she could eat—chickweed and nettle—and which to avoid. Some of the weeds tasted like garlic, and some were sour. "Yesterday, it was grasses with grains; today it's grains with grasses," Ona joked in her interview years later.

Still, hungry foragers made mistakes. Millions of people, not only deportees, became sick or disabled after eating toxic plants. When one Bielastok mother fell ill from a saltbush soup, a doctor prescribed as a cure three kilograms of flour, which could only be purchased with an official document. The prescription saved her.

Collective farm workers were paid in calories, according to daily production norms. Category One workers did not meet the farm's target production levels (Father Joseph, who did light work such as collecting horse bridles from field workers, belonged to this category); thus, they received the fewest rations—between 400 and 580 calories per day. This level of sustenance was insufficient to maintain bodily functions. Without the support of their fellow exiles, no Category One workers would have survived.

Hard labor combined with malnutrition caused many deported women to stop menstruating. The difficult conditions also delayed puberty for their daughters. "Where are you supposed to find the extra blood to give up?" one nurse explained to her troubled patients.

Category Two workers, or those who achieved between 100 and 150 percent of targeted production levels, received more rations. They were enough for the people to function but not to do much else.

Finally, there were the production heroes, the so-called Stakhanovites, who accomplished more than 150 percent of targets. They received superior rations as a reward.

Without exception, every Siberian who knew her described Ona as a "good worker" and an "award winner." Her rations would have been superior to those of the priest and the mothers with children. An agrarian childhood had prepared Ona for life in Siberia—especially in this part of it, where the land was arable and livestock plentiful—in ways that nothing else could have. She knew how to make laundry soap from ash and lye, to raise and slaughter pigs, to smoke and preserve meat, to pickle vegetables and preserve fruits, to milk a cow, to make cheese, to keep chickens, and to construct a root cellar. She could bake and cook with the most modest ingredients and create festive spreads for village celebrations. Never before had she considered these skills to be valuable or special; they came from her previous life, passed down from her grandmother and mother. But in Siberia they made her both a good diplomat and friend, and they raised her standing in the community.

In 1958, her final year in Siberia, Ona was honored as a *peredovik*, a "superior worker." Stalin and his successors distributed a myriad of medals for various achievements, including distinction in teaching, accomplished mothering, and courageous military service; for dedication in the cultivation of previously uncultivated lands; for the careful restoration of war-torn cities; and, evidently, for expert animal husbandry. Even deportees could earn such awards.

When my grandmother traveled to a conference in Tomsk to accept her prize, she left her young bovine charges for the first time. Despite Ona's assurances that the calves would come when called, the creatures missed their trusted and beloved caretaker. They wandered hungry and forlorn until her return.

27

Years after her return from exile, Ona only hinted at the emotional toll of the decades-long separation from her children. On the train to Siberia, she had felt no hunger, she said. All she had felt was numbness—or, I suppose, nothing at all. But in Brovka the loss of her family triggered an ache.

She and her children had no contact for six years. The first successful connection was both fleeting and one-sided. The postcard is a relic, its yellowing stock a witness to an improbable journey. It arrived in Germany in 1947, when Anthony and the three children were still living in a DP camp.

Before receiving the card, Ona's children had no idea if she was alive or dead or where she had disappeared. But that year mail started to travel between Siberia and Soviet Lithuania. Ona began to send news of her survival to her sister and to tell of her life in exile. Margarita reciprocated by telling Ona that her children had escaped to the West with their father.

But with diplomatic ties severed between Germany and the USSR, no mail could travel directly between the two enemy countries. Looking for a way to get word to her family, Ona remembered a cousin of Anthony's who lived in America. She wrote to her children care of him.

The postcard reads:

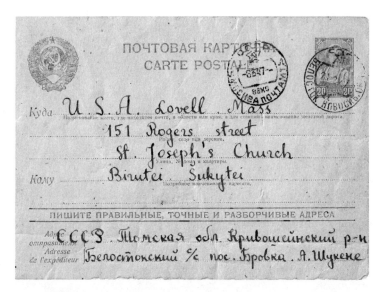

FIG. 27. Ona's postcard, 1947. Private collection. Courtesy of the author.

My Dear Children,

It made me indescribably happy to learn that you were alive and well. I'm healthy. I work on a farm. In my thoughts and in my heart I am always with you . . .

Your Mother

The year 1947 seems so early to me. Stalinism (along with Stalin himself) was still alive and well. It was the year Poland officially became a People's Republic. The year the Marshall Plan was born. The year they say the Cold War really began. It seems early until I remember that six years had already passed since Ona's deportation and that the little boy she had left behind was by then thirteen.

28

It was also in 1947 that a Forest Brother, code-named Aras (Eagle), was killed by the pro-Soviet paramilitary at the Lithuanian farm belonging to Margarita, Ona's sister, and her husband, Juozas. According to Soviet documents, this "bandit" had been a regular visitor there. The paramilitary claimed that Margarita's husband was a material and moral supporter of the armed resistance and specifically of Aras when he came to the farm. They arrested Juozas.

Further, in a gesture designed to humiliate both the living and the dead, they forced Juozas to sit atop Aras's corpse as he transported it by horse and carriage to the local marketplace, where he was ordered to dump it. Displaying mutilated bodies in public squares was common Soviet practice. Secret police could then see who recognized the dead or reacted with sorrow.

The Soviet courts sentenced Juozas to two years of hard labor in the Gulag, while Margarita was deported to a special settlement in Krasnoyarsk, a Siberian region some 600 kilometers east of Tomsk. Both were exiled from Lithuania in 1948.

Juozas survived his Gulag sentence, but Siberia's harsh climate, food shortages, and hard work all took their toll. He died shortly after joining his wife at her special settlement. Upon his death, Ona and Margarita petitioned for transfer on family reunification grounds. Initially, they asked that Ona be allowed to leave Brovka to join Margarita. The traces of this request highlight a rare moment of

FIG. 28. Juozas's Siberian grave, 1957. Private collection. Courtesy of the author.

humanity on the part of Soviet authorities: it was official policy to try to bring relatives back together whenever possible. The petitions attest that Margarita lived in the Siberian village of Yershovo alone and that she was unable to work. Included too are glowing character references for my grandmother. The government responded simply that it had no objection to the transfer.

In the end, it was Margarita who left her settlement to join Ona. There is no record as to how this change of plan came about, but in the autumn of 1954, the sisters set up house in Brovka together.

29

When Stalin died on March 5, 1953, the authorities embalmed his body and put it on public display at Lenin's Mausoleum in Moscow's Red Square. Millions of mourners came to view the tyrant's corpse. A great number of those visitors were sincere in their grief. In her biography of Stalin's daughter, Rosemary Sullivan cites a young Oleg Kalugin, who later became a general in the KGB:

> It is difficult for most people to imagine how a nation worshipped such a monster, but the truth is that most of us—those who had not felt the lash of his repression—did. We saw him as a man who led the country through the war, turned a backward nation into a superpower, built up our economy so that there was employment and housing and food enough for all. His propaganda machine was all-powerful . . . I revered Stalin.

But for Ona and other victims of Stalinist repression, the death of the tyrant was cause for celebration. Bielastok, for one, had suffered enormous losses under him. In 1938 the NKVD had gathered most of the hamlet's men and summarily executed them. Their crime, being Polish. Of some two hundred adult males, Stalin's men left only twenty alive. A monument to those murdered now stands in Bielastok, its inscription barely legible.

Nor had the Belarusians from across the river forgotten wartime outrages. When the potato crop had been poor and villagers were starving, Soviet tax collectors nevertheless seized 90 percent of the harvest. Households that failed to meet their quotas were made to supplement their payments with grain, even though it too was in short supply. Stalin himself conceived of this practice during his final 1928 trip to Siberia. He called it the "Urals method."

For those who had suffered through his terror, Stalin's painful death had an aspect of poetic justice. By 1953 the leader's paranoia and anti-Semitism had reached absurd levels. He saw enemies everywhere, even among his healers. Ironically, on the eve of his demise, Stalin had imprisoned the very men who could have saved his life. He had accused his doctors of conspiring against him in a Zionist plot; the imagined conspiracy was dubbed "The Doctors' Plot." And so it was that no medical help was on hand when he needed it.

Stalin lay in his dacha, paralyzed, unable to speak, and incontinent after an apparent stroke. By the eve of his death, he had isolated himself so completely that even his closest associates dared not intervene in any way for fear of being punished once their leader recovered. In the end, Stalin's daughter, Svetlana, watched as her father drowned in his bodily fluids, his face and lips blackening from a lack of oxygen. With one last glance and an outstretched hand, Joseph Stalin expired. Theories of murder, some more plausible than others, abound.

Few could imagine the changes this death would bring. In Brovka and Bielastok, Ona heard people cursing Stalin openly, but she never believed they would get away with it. The loosening of speech must be a ploy, she thought, a ruse to prompt more arrests. Like so many others, she never dared show her joy at Stalin's demise.

But things did change and quickly. Soon, all fifteen men accused in the Doctors' Plot were released and declared innocent. Next, in an unprecedented move, the Ministry of the Interior released a statement that evidence against the men had been fabricated and the doctors' confessions extracted through torture. This was a sign of changes to come, a precursor to Nikolai Khrushchev's Thaw.

In his first year in power, Stalin's successor, Khrushchev, led the USSR to major criminal reforms and decreed broad amnesties, releasing 48 percent of the Gulag population. A million people found themselves freed in one fell swoop. They included prisoners with sentences of fewer than five years, pregnant women, and mothers with children under the age of ten. That was only the beginning. Ultimately, between April 1953 (one month after Stalin's death) and January 1956, the Gulag population decreased by 66 percent.

But freedom came with challenges. Deportees and ex-prisoners faced an uphill battle when they returned home. In the minds of those they'd left behind, they remained "bandits," "gangsters," and "enemies of the people." Many found themselves both jobless and homeless. Some grew so desperate that they committed offenses (like posting anti-Soviet leaflets on ministry buildings) to ensure their rearrest and a return to the camps.

In Lithuania, it was not until the post-Soviet period of the 1990s and the publication of groundbreaking memoirs of Siberian exile that the public's attitude toward returnees began to shift significantly. Exile suddenly became a badge of honor, a mark of martyrdom, so even those who had never set foot near the Urals wanted a piece of that distinction. Fueled by the groundswell of national pride and support for the independence movement, a "myth of 'universal' deportation" appeared. According to this myth, all Lithuanians were deportees, removed if not from their land, then from their language and culture. It's easy to imagine how a nonmetaphorical deportee like Ona—one whose actual body traveled east across the tundra and back—might find such a recasting of exile questionable.

With her sentence of twenty years, my grandmother did not benefit from Khrushchev's first amnesty. Her sister Margarita, it seems, may have—almost. According to Ministry of the Interior documents, she received permission to leave Siberia in 1956, but then this permission, for reasons unknown, was revoked. It would be another two years before both women regained a modicum of their former freedom.

30

After three years of sleeping communally with six others and more than a decade living with a Belarusian family, Ona managed to procure a house in Brovka for her final years of exile. The log cabin she shared with Margarita stood beyond the village, past where its paved road now ends. Today, a sprawling new building, filled with dairy cows as in Ona's day, stands in place of the Soviet-era kolkhoz.

Darius and I followed Evdonia Vasilevna Bielyaskaya, or "Dusya," as she invited us to call her, down the winding dirt road and back up the hill. For a time, Dusya had lived in the house Ona built and then left behind. I knew we wouldn't see my grandmother's Siberian home. The cabin, only a stone's throw from the farm, had been demolished several decades before to make way for a new calving facility. After its razing, no building ever went up in its place, and no trace of it remains. Still, I wanted to see the site.

As we approached the farm, we could smell the cows, and Dusya remarked that it had been impossible to live at Ona's old place because of the odors. *But apparently not for Ona*, I thought with an edge of bitterness I didn't quite understand. But my mood quickly shifted when Dusya stopped before an open field and gestured out to a pasture. "It was there," she said. "You see those trees? That's where the garden was."

FIG. 29. Ona's Siberian house, 1958. Private collection. Courtesy of the author.

FIG. 30. Julija on Brovka's ridge, 2010. Courtesy of the author.

Across the stream from the kolkhoz and Ona's fallow garden plot, nothing of Brovka remains except a roll in the landscape. Brush and bramble have taken the former village's place, and grasses have reclaimed what were once the yards of both exiles and native-born Siberians. I found no trace of the Belarusian couple and their daughter or of my grandmother who had followed calves and sheep back and forth across these meadows. But the flowers all around grew from the seeds of the seeds of the seeds that had brushed onto Ona's pants as she walked. The flies that buzzed around my face were distant relatives of those that Agnieszka had swatted with her tail. And the Siberian sky that stretched all around was the same one Ona searched at night for stars.

Brovka was no longer. But here, at last, was I. And here, at last, was Darius, the boy Ona had raised.

Before turning back for the village, I picked up three stones: two mottled white and gray, one black. They were plain, unremarkable. Jagged and unpoetic, the stones traveled home with me and now sit atop a bookshelf beside the stone from the Newtown cemetery. I thought about the Tomsk nuclear accident as I slipped those pebbles into my pocket and wondered if rocks absorbed radioactivity. I even searched the Internet for an answer to this question upon my return home, but I found no answer.

What else might these stones have absorbed? How many exiles, young and old, had kicked them? How many hooves had scuffed them? How many Russian boys destined for deaths far too early had used them to invent games of chance and skill?

31

The sisters' log cabin featured an iron stove, thatched roof, and unpainted wooden floors. The house itself was small, with a single room for sleeping, cooking, writing, reading, sewing, sleeping, chatting with friends who came with news, and doing everything else that happens in a home. Each spring, once the last of the snow had finally melted, Ona and Margarita lined the walls with a new layer of newspaper. And every autumn, the sisters filled their root cellar with potatoes, onions, and grain. In summer, poppies surrounding the house stood tall enough to graze Ona's hips.

A 1957 photograph shows Margarita at the cabin's edge. She's swarthy, dark-haired, and wearing an apron as she gazes ahead of her, severe looking. By contrast, Ona—fair-haired and apronless in a black dress—stands smack in the middle of the image. Two windows flank her as she squints and smiles directly at the camera. She folds her arms as if taking stock of her own power.

Unseen on the table inside the log cabin lie a pair of glasses—a legacy of Margarita's late husband—awaiting that evening's correspondence. The sisters shared that single pair of spectacles to write. First one sister would compose her letters and then hand the glasses to the other so she could write. The language in the many missives Ona penned is folksy yet precise and impressively strong for one with so little formal education. Margarita, however, writes without punctuation, like this: *without taking a breath her*

FIG. 31. Margarita and Ona among the poppies outside their cabin, 1957. Private collection. Courtesy of the author.

sentences run on until she has finished what she has to say even if this means stringing several disjointed ideas together and the reader must work hard to find where to stop and take a pause.

Anthony's first letter arrived in Brovka in 1955. The Bradford postmark and the letter from her faraway family were so unexpected that Ona had to go to the farm's medical center to recover. She later wrote to her children that she'd suffered a heart attack, but I imagine what she actually experienced was shock. In my mind's eye I see her sit down to write that first reply, smoothing the paper before her. After dating it carefully, she lifts her eyes, puts down her pen and then the glasses. Ona sits like this for hours, late into the night. Finally, with a deep breath, she picks up the spectacles and starts her response.

I do not need to imagine the letter. It, along with many others, came to me after Ona's death.

MAY 1, 1955. BROVKA.

Anthony!

I received your letter on May 1. It made me indescribably happy. I'm healthy, alive, and I live together with my sister Margarita. She moved in with me last fall. Her husband is dead. Margarita's two daughters live in Lithuania with their husbands and children.

I'm working on a farm raising calves.

Spring has arrived here as well; the rivers are carrying the ice away. In some areas, layers of snow remain.

Best wishes to you and your little ones, who remain in my mind's eye every day.

I await your next letter with impatience.

I kiss you all.

At least twice a month for five years, Ona wrote to her children from her Siberian log house. She told of raising animals at the farm, haying, and chopping firewood. She described how Margarita; with her chronic bronchitis, stayed home and did "woman's work." In December 1956 she wrote:

Days go by quite quickly. I don't do anything at home. Godmother [Margarita] takes care of everything. Once I finish my work on the farm I bring home some firewood or some hay for Agnieszka. Haying is fun at first, but bringing it home will drive you to tears. Of course, this is the case for women without men. I often wonder how it would be if my men, my strong oaks, were here. But what can I do, if this is how fate wanted it for me?

The world Ona portrayed for her children was one of hard work (eighteen-hour days), of snow and ice ("in our garden you can just see the tops of the hay stacks"), of small pleasures ("those little slippers are like a dream, so cuddly and light"), and of life close to the land. She wrote of joyful harvests:

The potatoes grew very big, despite the fact that they froze in the spring. The earth renews them, and it keeps raining, which is good for them.

She also shared news of occasional festivities:

In a couple of days we will celebrate the October Revolution. The collective farm is planning a party. They're making beer. It's going to be great.

Just as important as the human cast of characters and, in some ways, perhaps even more so were the animals Ona and Margarita kept privately. There was Agnieszka the cow, Baltis the pig, and the chickens that lived inside the house during winter. Ona treasured the animals but not sentimentally. Their purpose was clear: they were life sustaining and had to be slaughtered. Only one rooster and a chicken that Ona was symbolically raising for her granddaughter (my eldest cousin) in Canada, whom she had never met, were safe and the subject of regular updates:

You ask what we feed the pigs and the chickens—potatoes and grain, of course. We slaughtered our roosters, but granddaughter's little rooster and chicken are growing. This year, the rooster isn't as necessary since we have a clock. The chickens are already sitting under the stove: it's cold in the barn.

Ona was not an educated woman. A farmer's daughter, under different circumstances, she would have left no trace.

Her stories are a reminder of countless other lives like hers, the thousands upon thousands of people who were forced to travel across the steppes. Some strove to return and found their way home. Many didn't. Some of their tales have been recorded and safeguarded, while others have been lost as the tellers died, as the languages of grandmothers were forgotten by their grandchildren and great-grandchildren in the West, and as the attics were cleaned out and boxes of letters like Ona's discarded. Although Ona had probably always been a storyteller, exile made her a writer. And my grandmother wrote for a very specific audience, her children. They were by now adult children, to be sure (by the time Siberian exiles were allowed to correspond with the West—this happened only after Stalin's death—her youngest child, my father, was twenty years old). For Ona, though, they had not aged.

> Not long ago I dreamt about everyone. You were all school-aged. I can never see you as you are now, my dear children.

An audience of children requires a narrative appropriate for children, so Ona created a Brovka that seemed to be a magical winter wonderland, where women dashed off on sleighs to pick up parcels, where they told each other's fortunes with playing cards, where they bathed in saunas, where they dressed in pink long underwear before venturing outside to have their eyelashes promptly stick together from the cold, where all creatures had names, and where the walls of houses were papered in letters, pressed flowers, and drawings that arrived from overseas.

Disasters, such as Ona's teeth getting knocked out when a steel rod broke free from a combine harvester, were mentioned only in passing (with reassurances that the teeth had fallen out painlessly). Questions from the children about the hardships of the journey from Lithuania to Siberia were dealt with briefly and in scant detail:

> You ask about the journey and how long we traveled. It took about two weeks. First we stopped in the Altai region, we hadn't been there for long when we carried on, I don't know why. I like it here much better. The land is excellent and it's rich in forests and fields. It's just that the summer is short and the winter is long.

The letters did not talk about the political reality of the time or about life under collectivization but recounted instead scenes of weddings with the Siberian brides being adorned with homemade veils of muslin and paper, of tasting homebrew that was all the rage, of cinema night at the kolkhoz, of the changing seasons, and of the passage of time.

The Siberian letters have both delighted and discouraged me. On the one hand, they are vivid portraits of Ona's tiny life on the

Siberian plain. But on the other hand, silence, absence, suppression, and even self-censorship lie over the letters like a veil, obscuring essential pieces of the past. I can see and experience Ona's Siberia through her letters but only partially and sometimes only in silhouette. Ultimately, I have come to accept the distance. I have no other choice.

32

On my last night in Bielastok, I ducked into a backyard kitchen house to wash off the dust from the walk with Dusya. There, the most beautiful sight of my Siberian trip greeted me. Two swallows circled a bare light bulb hanging in the middle of the room. One bird then darted out the door, while the other perched itself on a piece of cardboard nestled in the corner behind a pile of potatoes. A starchy and earthy scent of fermenting tubers filled the air.

Whenever I entered our host's kitchen house over those Siberian days, I could never decide whether the smell that confronted me there was good or bad. Sweet, yes, but it was a bit sickly too. The odor has stayed with me as a memory. Months after my return home, I opened the door to my own kitchen cupboard to discover a soggy bag of rotting potatoes. The smell of Siberia hit me hard and caught in the back of my throat. For a moment, I was back in Bielastok.

The swallow and I watched each other for a few seconds. Silently, I bid it safe travels and held my breath as it flew out the door to join its companion.

In Ona's case, it was 1956 before she began seriously considering the possibility of leaving Siberia and hopefully reuniting with her children. A photograph taken that year shows her standing before a white curtain; one hand is behind her back and the other down at her side. She wears a dark polka-dot dress with a smart white collar, thick tights, and mannish laced shoes. Her hair is pulled back. Though she wears a dress in almost every Siberian photograph I've seen, I know from her letters that she didn't don dresses regularly in exile. If women did opt for dresses on the farms and special settlements of Siberia, they pulled trousers on underneath them to protect themselves from the insects or the cold, depending on the season. The elderly women I saw and met in Siberia still dress this way.

In the photograph Ona is sunburned from haying and walking in the fields with grazing calves. Between tending animals, cultivating her vegetable garden, chopping wood, and carrying water, my grandmother must have spent most of every Siberian day outside.

On December 16, 1956, she wrote to her children optimistically of her initial inquiries regarding her return. In her letter she uses the word "vacation" as a euphemism for her return to Lithuania. Before even dreaming of joining her family overseas, Ona first had to secure permission to leave Siberia.

> Yesterday I talked to a big "uncle." He said that I definitely have to get "vacation" first, and only then can I start on identification papers. Once I've spent some time "on vacation" (about half a year), I should be able to attain the goal of seeing my children. But sitting here, I won't accomplish anything. He told me where I needed to submit the request, and that I would get it for sure. Once I get the time, I can stay here if I want. No one will force me to leave. So, one day soon, I'll send a request to Moscow.

Ona's file from the Ministry of the Interior records her doggedness. My grandmother sent letter after letter and request after request that her name be removed from the list of special settlers and that she be allowed to rejoin her children. The correspondence chain, similar to the one that resulted in Margarita's transfer to Brovka, begins with a character reference dated March 3, 1958. It's stamped with the seal of the Voroshilov Collective Farm:

> Since 1942 she has been working in livestock production. Each year, the kolkhoz administration and the District Executive Committee

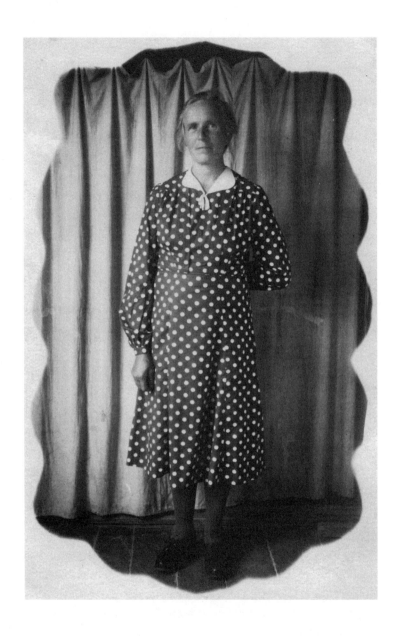

FIG. 32. Ona in the polka-dot dress, 1956. Private collection. Courtesy of the author.

have presented her with valuable gifts for her honest work. In 1958, because of her production results of 1957, Ona was chosen to participate in the conference of top workers in agriculture that took place in Tomsk.

In April 1957 Ona wrote to Kliment Voroshilov—chairman of the Presidium of the Supreme Soviet, close associate of Stalin's, and namesake of her collective farm—asking that he allow her either to join her family in England or to return to Lithuania. On September 17, 1957, came news that her request had been received and refused. More denials in 1957 bookend this one: May 11, May 25, October 31, November 27, and December 19. "My 'dad' won't let me go," Ona wrote to her children in England. "He will never agree." The official letters offer no grounds for the decision, only that there is "no reason" to end her exile.

Her determination to be reunited with her family, which is apparent in Ona's Soviet file, belies a frustration found in her letters. This one dates from October 9, 1956:

> You write that you see me in your dreams with sagging socks. It may well be that when Moscow replies, my socks will fall! I don't know what will happen, but I have this feeling of hopelessness. I often dream about all of you as well. Not long ago, I dreamed of Anthony, I think we met at some sort of get-together. I was so happy to have found him that I took him by the hand and said "finally, at least this once it's not a dream." When I told him that I only saw him in my sleep, he looked unhappy and wouldn't talk. Why are there so many misunderstandings in dreams? You two girls are always school-aged when I dream about you. I never see you as you are now.

In early 1958 she tried another approach. Instead of appealing for her release on family reunification grounds, she submitted evidence of her deteriorating health. Her conditions included myocardiodystrophy, emphysema, rheumatic polyarthritis ("my health is still holding strong, except that sometimes all my limbs hurt," she wrote to her kids), and chronic gastritis. Again Ona received the answer that there was "no reason" to release her since she could still perform "light duties." She wrote,

Almost every month people from here and from there are leaving on vacation, while I sit here as if nailed to the ground. It's very unsettling. I often think that I can't possibly be that much worse than all the rest. It can't be.

The Soviet files confirm that no charges had ever been filed against her. She received no official account of the authorities' decisions either to deport her or to keep her in Siberia. When asked why she'd been exiled, Ona could give no answer. The collective farm's foreman (whom she liked very much) once asked the question, and all she could do was turn it gently back on him. "You tell me," she said. "Perhaps you have some evidence against me? What did I do? I don't feel guilty of anything."

33

On July 10, 1958, Ona received word that her name had finally been removed from the registry of special settlements. Her release had nothing to do with her numerous letters and documents. It was most likely the result of the policy shift under Khrushchev. The effects of the blanket pardon of all exiles had finally reached my grandmother. She was one of eighty thousand people—twenty thousand from the Gulags and sixty thousand from special settlements—who returned to Lithuania between 1953 and 1970. The only condition for receiving permission to go home was that she sign a document renouncing her confiscated property and her rights to the apartment from which she had been deported.

But in August 1958, instead of celebrating, the sisters spent their last Siberian days in sorrow. Margarita's son-in-law had died suddenly and unexpectedly, and she wanted to return to her daughters in Lithuania as quickly as possible. Ona sold off everything in a hurry, including her beloved cow, Agnieszka. Because she could not delay her journey, she didn't get a fair price for the cow. Her one-eared cat (whose pinna had frozen and fallen off one winter, Ona explained) wouldn't come down from the roof, so she had to leave it where it stood.

The details of Ona's and Margarita's hasty departure reached England in the form of a letter.

AUGUST 12, 1958

My Dear Children!

Yesterday we received such a sad, almost unbearable letter from Godmother's daughter in Lithuania, whose words are even hard to repeat. I am enclosing that widow's letter, God forbid that anything like this happen to anyone else. Godmother won't stop sobbing, and it's difficult to comfort her. She keeps asking what she will find when she returns. A widow and orphans. Why are we faced with such torrents of tears? We always talked about how joyful it would be when we returned: we would celebrate, the children would come meet us at the station, and we would visit the rest of the family. Now, our palace of thoughts has crumbled. As they say here, our thoughts are a year ahead of us and death is at our shoulders. Godmother's son-in-law will no longer greet us.

At the daughter's request we're going to leave as soon as possible. My plan had been to depart from here around September 20. Everything is growing wonderfully in the garden, and I didn't want to leave it for someone else for next to nothing. I had planned to harvest a little early and to take it to the purchasing station for a reasonable price. But because Margarita's daughter has written like this, asking her mother to return, I can't torture them anymore. I'll sell what I can, however I can. I will sell Agnieszka to the *kolkhoz*. She was so difficult to acquire, yet here she is, so easy to sell, especially at a reduced price. It's hard to say when we will leave, though we'll try to go as quickly as possible. We'll take a steamboat from Krivosheino to Tomsk, which will take about 15–16 hours. Then in Tomsk we'll get a ticket all the way to Kaunas. We will only need to transfer in Moscow. It takes four days and four nights to travel from Tomsk to Moscow. From Moscow we'll travel a day and a night to Kaunas. They say that there's a very long line at Tomsk for tickets. People wait 8–10 days.

I received your letters a long time ago. It's nice to read happy letters and to take pleasure in my children's successes. But the sorrowful letter from Lithuania has knocked me off my life's track. My dear children, don't write to me at this address anymore, instead write to me at Godmother's daughter's house in Lithuania. I think I'll stay there for a while as well. Oh yes, we've already made a deal to sell our house for 2,500. Godmother is finding and sewing bags for our parcels. Let's hope that this letter will be your last visitor from this cold country, and bearing such painful news, my dear God.

I kiss you all with tears in my eyes. I'm with you in my thoughts and in my heart.

Your Mother

The letter from Margarita's daughter in Lithuania and with the details of the sorrowful news has perished, but its memory remains.

Ona's elder daughter told me that Margarita's son-in-law had been a chauffeur in Lithuania; his job was to drive officials around the country. One rainy day, he drove a car onto a ferry that crossed the Nemunas River in Kaunas. The ship's deck was slippery, and the son-in-law slid off the ferry's edge and into the river's frigid waters to his death.

34

Whether she knew it or not, Ona was the wife of a wanted man. Indeed, her husband remained a wanted man long after Stalin's death. His search file was only closed in 1985, the year Anthony died. As nonsensical as it seems, Ona herself was considered an enemy of the people, not only by authorities, but also by a great number of the ordinary folks she met when she returned home. In Soviet Lithuania, she found herself without a place to live, so she divided her time between the farm where her sister and nieces resided and a small apartment in Kaunas that belonged to in-laws.

For money, she was reduced to selling scarves and nylon stockings that her daughters sent from the West. Ona would have been fifty-three when she returned to Lithuania, but she was not yet of retirement age. Having worked "only" seventeen years on the farm, she was three years short of the twenty years required for a pension.

Marginal and suspect, Ona thus eked out a life and waited, as she wrote in a letter dated November 25, 1961, for "a droplet of grace." If she missed the wide-open land, friends, and animals of Brovka, she didn't say so, but in these letters, Soviet Lithuania seems dark, cold, and cramped. She often found herself stuck on the nieces' farm and longing for the city.

She wrote from the soggy countryside on December 6, 1961:

The weather's worsened. It rained a lot and churned up a great mess of mud. And once again it's a problem to be caught out with no rubber boots. I can't even leave the front yard. I always leave Kaunas most unwillingly, but I don't want to overstay my welcome there or take up too much space.

Around the corner from the tiny apartment she shared with four others when visiting her beloved city, the nearby baroque cathedral offered Ona daily refuge.

Once again, my grandmother threw herself into the task of navigating the Soviet bureaucracy, trying to secure permission to leave the country and join her children:

I must admit that I have no sense that I'll be successful in leaving this place for all those comforts. Such good fortune is not mine to have.

The tone of these Lithuanian letters is darker and sadder than that of the Siberian ones. Now Ona seems more acutely aware of the passage of time and of opportunities lost with each day:

If only we could spend one more Christmas Eve together. Here we are again. Another Christmas, and I'm alone as always. They'll keep us waiting until we close our eyes and our lives are done. The years roll by like apples. Time runs without ever stopping, and we'll have long since grown old.

35

Seven years passed for Ona in Soviet Lithuania until, in 1965, she decided to change her strategy. She followed the example of a fellow exile, whom she called a "friend in suffering," and went to Moscow.

I imagine that the metropolis would have overwhelmed Ona, with its broad boulevards and majestic subway stations. It would certainly have dwarfed both Tomsk and Vilnius, the two largest cities she had ever visited before then. Thankfully, she had friends in Moscow. She knew a young party official, a Siberian who lived and worked in the Soviet capital. He had returned to his village to marry a local girl, and Ona had been a guest at their wedding. She decided to go and seek out his help.

Ona recounted the episode in the 1977 interview whose transcript I found in the archives:

> I didn't know that he was such a good person. He agreed to see me that same day. He accompanied me, saying that it was impossible to find anything at those offices. So we went up to the little window of the Ministry of the Interior. The clerk there said that the minister wasn't in. He was in a meeting and would return to the office only at two o'clock. He told us to wait. When the time came, my companion stayed in the waiting room. The minister invited me into his office and I started talking.

"What did you come here for," he asked me. "Vilnius takes care of all this."

At this point I didn't call him "Comrade." Instead I said "Chief."

"Chief," I said, "what am I supposed to make of this? Every time I go to Vilnius, I always get the answer: Moscow takes care of all this. Where can I find justice?" I told him, "I think that my fate is in your hands."

Then I showed him my prize certificate, the one I got for my work with those animals. It said I was conscientious, so I started to talk about that.

"I got this prize," I said.

"From the *kolkhoz*?" he asked.

"Yes," I said. And I took the certificate and put it down in front of him. "Chief," I said, "I worked seventeen years for the Soviet Union." I said this truthfully.

Then he asked me: "Are you alone? Where are your children?"

"It was Stalin's era," I told him. "There were deportations. They deported me. I spent seventeen years working conscientiously for the Soviet Union. I've returned to Lithuania."

He asked: "Are you working?"

"I'm not working."

"Do you receive a pension?"

"No, I don't receive anything."

"So what do you live on?"

I say: "I live on these rags. Is it easy for me, Chief," I say, "to live from those rags? Having worked this many years for the Soviet Union?"

He says, "Invite your children here."

"I don't have anything to offer them," I say. "I live as a guest with a relative. She gave me a corner. There's a room with a bed, and under that bed is my suitcase. I have nothing to offer."

He says, "We will give them apartments. We will give them jobs."

"Originally, there were three children," I tell him. "But now there are ten family members. If one comes," (I can't say this very boldly) "perhaps, one of them would come . . . But I'm a mother, I want to

FIG. 33. Ona leaving Lithuania for Canada, 1965. Private collection. Courtesy of the author.

see them all. Chief," I say, "is it easier for me to go there alone, or for all of them to come here?"

As I was talking I could feel tears flowing down my cheeks.

"Chief, my fate is in your hands. If you say yes, I will go. If you say no, then I'm buried alive."

And then like a miracle . . .

36

By the 1960s, all three of my grandmother's children had emigrated to Canada. Ona hoped to make it there in time to see her son marry, but it was not to be. Perhaps because they simply wanted to get on with their lives, or because there was little hope she would ever actually arrive, the young couple (my parents) went ahead with their plans in her absence.

One night in 1965, while eating dinner with his new wife at his Toronto home, my father received a call from Canadian Embassy officials. His mother was on a plane to Canada, that person informed him, and she would arrive at Toronto's airport in a matter of hours.

No account of how that first meeting went is very detailed, but they all indicate there was a great deal of confusion. Ona missed her connection in Montreal, and the scramble to find her seems to have dulled other emotions. Her eldest granddaughter, then a young girl, said that, above all, it was Ona's odor that struck her the first time she met our grandmother. Ona had been carrying a sausage in her handbag, nibbling at it over her multiday journey from Kaunas to Vilnius to Moscow and across the Atlantic. A nub remained, and its sweaty, meaty scent overpowered the granddaughter.

"She smelled like Russia," my cousin said, opening her eyes wide.

Though I doubt she ever voiced it to her children, my grandmother found the reunion with them disorienting. In the 1977 Chicago interview, she recounted how while on her 1958 trip from Brovka to Lithuania, Ona had stopped in Moscow for a day to visit a Siberian-born girl named Tanya, the daughter of the elderly Belarusian couple she'd lived with in Brovka. Ona loved this young woman in part because she reminded her of her own elder daughter. Tanya had married and moved from Brovka to the Soviet capital with her new husband. I suspect he was the same man who later accompanied my grandmother to the Ministry of the Interior. In any case, when Ona arrived in Moscow en route from Siberia, the young couple greeted her at the train station and took her home to a meal of roast chicken, cognac, and cakes.

"It was like coming home to family," Ona said many years later, comparing the two reunions. "We were so happy, we cried. I felt more at home with those Siberian Muscovites than I did with my own children. When I met my children after so many years, we were strangers."

All these years after the war, when Ona finally arrived in Canada, Anthony was still living in a Bradford rowhouse. He'd never believed the Soviets would allow his wife to leave the USSR, so he refused to consider preparing for her arrival until her feet had touched Canadian soil. Once they had, Anthony put his property up for sale and began to make arrangements to emigrate. A year later, Anthony crossed the Atlantic to join Ona.

On the plane heading back from Tomsk to Moscow and then on to Frankfurt, where we parted, Darius and I talked about our family and about the sadness and misfortune that have visited us with a terrible frequency. Both my father and his mother, Ona's two younger children, died suddenly and unexpectedly—he of a heart attack when I was eighteen and she six years later of a cancer that killed her in a matter of weeks.

They had escaped deportation, but did it nevertheless kill them as adults? I wondered aloud. Had the loss of their mother in childhood damaged them so severely that it shortened their lives? Did my father literally die of a broken heart and Darius's mother of a wound that festered until it finally transformed itself into a cancer? Was Ona's eldest child more resilient than her younger siblings, somehow sturdier, and thus better able to withstand the shock?

"I don't know," Darius said. "I never thought of it that way."

PART III

Us

37

When I first read them, the eyewitness statements and details outlined in Anthony's search file knocked the breath out of me. Months went by before I could bring myself to write a couple of email inquiries to historians, asking for advice on how to read the files. More than a year passed before I could speak to friends of what I'd discovered. I feared they would see me differently if they knew the truth of my origins. Already, it had changed the way I saw myself.

But when I finally worked up my courage, told my tale, and described my reaction to the KGB files, I found that friends struggled to understand why the revelations had affected me so profoundly. When I confessed that I'd been wrestling with the idea that I might carry responsibility for what happened in Newtown, they all dismissed the notion out of hand.

"It has nothing to do with you," they each said without fail.

But it does, because somebody always pays.

Ona paid with the loss of her children, her homeland, and her middle years. My father and his sisters paid with the loss of their mother. I pay too, just by knowing. These discoveries have been poisonous, a bitter pill to swallow.

I've even wondered, over these months of writing, if certain facts are better left undiscovered. Would it have been preferable for me to live out my life ignorant of what Anthony is accused of having done in Newtown?

Ona had this much luck at least, I thought. *She couldn't possibly have known about the accusations against Anthony.* But as I began discussing the matter with friends, I found that most of them disagreed with me on that point as well.

"Postwar Lithuania was all about gossip and innuendo," said my world-weary friend L——. "If she didn't know anything when she returned to Lithuania in 1958, acquaintances and perhaps foes would have filled her in before long. And in the process of leaving the USSR in 1965, she would have had a series of exit interviews with Soviet authorities. Surely, one of those officials let the cat out of the bag at some point."

Anthony's crime was an overlooked stain upon the family's peace. A contaminant impossible to purify, like ants in sugar.

38

How did they return to one another? How much did they share of what had happened in the other's absence? How did they pick up the thread of their marriage? For me, these are among the biggest mysteries of my grandparents' story. When I asked what it was like for her parents to reunite after so many years, my aunt—the eldest of the three siblings—shook her head and said she'd never posed such questions. But I wonder. Did they talk about what they'd seen, heard, and done in their years apart, or did they just live from moment to moment? Was there tenderness between them? Did they still love one another? I have no idea.

Darius described our grandparents as living a peaceful if seemingly separate existence, coming together for church, meals, and family events.

"They rarely touched," he said.

Other deportees saw their families crumble under the pressure of distance and terror. Years of forced separation tore innumerable unions apart. Male returnees remarried more readily than female ones did. Some men started over with younger women. Some found love with other returnees, to whom they felt bound by common experience. Though reunions, like that of my grandparents, "ranged from happy to tragic," there were nonetheless "countless instances of long marital faithfulness."

For her part, Ona's elder daughter is certain that Anthony never had another woman in his life. I, for my part, believe Ona was celibate the whole time she was in Siberia. If either Ona or Anthony were full of rage, neither showed it. Nor did they hint at regret, guilt, or remorse.

But sometimes Ona showed signs of sorrow. Shortly after reaching Canada, she traveled to Los Angeles to visit her third and youngest sister, Regina, who had arrived in the United States as a postwar refugee with their mother. By 1965 their mother was dead. Regina took her sister to visit the grave. The women arrived to find the cemetery's sprinklers working, so they had to wait a long time before paying their respects. Regina, who loved margaritas, wore huge sunglasses, drove a big car, and followed college sports on TV, grew antsy and bored. Tensions mounted between the sisters, but Ona was adamant. They would wait.

By the time she'd made her way across the grass, Ona's feet were soaked. Standing before her mother's grave, she broke down in sobs. Regina, frightened by Ona's grief, ushered her sister out of the cemetery, promising to return. They never did. Regina had decided that another visit would be too much for Ona to handle.

39

Starting in 1966 my grandparents lived in a small apartment building, where Anthony worked as the superintendent in return for
rent. Their apartment had wooden floors, a narrow, dark corridor,
and yellow walls. The building's long balconies framed an inner
courtyard.

In the thirty-one years she spent in Canada, Ona never learned
to speak English. Though on Sundays she attended the Lithuanian-
language Mass at the tiny Saint Catharine's community parish, on
weekdays—even though she couldn't understand the service—she
went to hear Mass in English in the city's cathedral. She sat in the
same pew, relative to the altar, as she had in Kaunas after her return
from Siberia. Soon, the local priest grew curious about this daily
visitor and approached her. As she always did when addressed in
English, my grandmother responded with a smile and a chuckle,
then went on her way.

In Canada, as in Siberia, she loved to cook. But on this side of
the Atlantic, food was plentiful and the possibilities endless. She
made the kitchen table groan with potato pancakes, waffle torts,
roasts, salads, and home-fermented pickles. She had time for other
pleasures too. The evenings Darius visited, they would watch the
Carol Burnett Show together. Ona would laugh and laugh at the
physical comedy. And when it was the season, she loved to follow
hockey on TV.

Darius described Saturday mornings in the 1970s, when, after spending the night in her apartment, he would run to Ona's room and climb under the covers to cuddle. It was the only time she felt soft, he said. Her huge breasts would fall to one side and her belly to the other. At all other times, she felt hard because of the corset she wore to support her back, which had been ruined by years of hard work in Siberia.

Anthony was there too, of course. Every night, sitting in a leather recliner and cupping his ear to catch the television's sound better, he watched Walter Cronkite read the news. And he slept in the single bed beside his wife's.

But Ona was the center of my cousin's childhood. Darius regularly went shopping with our grandmother or to hear concerts with her at the park bandstand.

Meanwhile, I remember feeling shy and nervous about going out in public with our grandmother. The idea of her circulating with no understanding of the language all around terrified me. I couldn't imagine how she coped and was constantly afraid of wounding her somehow.

40

In her garden beside the apartment building, Ona had a little shed that you could see from her bedroom window and that she'd fixed up like the Siberian backyard kitchen house in which I watched the swallows circle. There, we once prepared a cake together. When we began to mix ingredients in a bowl and added sugar, I drew in my breath, quick. Black dots punctuated the clean, white mound of crystals. Stored in the shed, the sugar had attracted insects, which now crawled over our fixings. I looked at my grandmother, expecting her to toss the mixture or at least to gasp as I had. She did neither. Instead, she simply continued to make the cake.

As she stirred and chatted, I sat in silence and watched, unsure of what to do. Perhaps she hadn't seen the ants. Should I tell her? Point them out?

But at that moment, as in the years that followed, something powerful silenced me. I suspect I remained quiet because I didn't want to be the girl who was too fancy to eat a few insects, sensing that Ona had eaten far, far worse in her life.

Many years later, this childhood hunch was confirmed. In the 1977 interview, Ona was asked about the availability of fresh, clean water in Siberia. "Were there wells?" the journalist inquired.

"Yes, but we would go out to the fields for entire days, and it was impossible to carry enough water." They drank from whatever sources were available, she explained, including puddles. "I was lying on my belly drinking," she continued, "when I noticed a cow turd. It had been hard and dry at one point, but then it had rained and the shit dissolved into the puddle. Only once I'd finished drinking did I notice."

The interviewer groaned. Ona laughed.

41

Our family gatherings tended to be formal and dominated by adult conversation, so asking about my grandmother's exile would have seemed inappropriate or even rude. While she was still alive, I squirreled away what Siberian crumbs she offered, but I never actively solicited more substantial pieces of her story. By the time I was in my late teens and ready to ask, Ona was incapable of answering. She'd become lost inside her head, unable to keep track of time, place, or people.

Whenever we visited her at the nursing home, Ona told the same stories over and over: how she'd been so embarrassed by her height as a young girl in Lithuania that she'd tried to look shorter by exaggeratedly bending her knees as she walked, how the one-eared cat had refused to come down from the roof the day she'd left Brovka, and how the mosquitoes there had been so thick that she'd used a rag to wipe them off her face. Some Siberian days, Ona must have said a thousand times or more, had been so cold that if you spat in the air, your saliva froze before it hit the ground. A writer I know claims to have tried this at minus fifty degrees in South Dakota. It didn't work, he said. He claimed Jack London had invented the detail for one of his stories. I wonder how my grandmother would have responded to that.

While she was still well enough, she used to go on annual mushroom-hunting trips in the southern Ontario forests with fellow parishioners from the Lithuanian church and their Lithuanian priest. On one of these occasions, she shared with her pastor some stories about the cold and mosquitoes of Siberia. "Oh, go on," the priest replied, "it couldn't possibly have been that bad. You're exaggerating."

The comment cut her. Short of her own children's lack of faith, this clergyman's accusation that she was somehow untruthful was perhaps the most hurtful thing she could imagine. In the dementia of her last years, the tales of battling Siberian insects were joined by the endlessly repeated anecdote of the doubtful priest.

In 1990, at my father's funeral, I held Ona's hand during the Mass. By then, her grip on the present had fallen away entirely. She could remember nothing from one moment to the next. Again and again, she asked me who had died and immediately forgot my answer. Again and again, I told her she'd lost her youngest child. Shock and sorrow hit her with equal force each time. It was almost unbearable to witness.

Ona herself died six years after her son and only two weeks before cancer took her middle child, Darius's mother. I suppose it's a small blessing and consolation that she didn't have to see a second child buried. Darius, for one, was thankful for that.

But fate couldn't leave well enough alone. In a final insult, standing over Ona's casket to utter the closing words on her life was the priest who had accused her of exaggerating the life she'd lived in Siberia.

42

For forty years, it seems, I have overvalued my origins. All my life, I have put so much stock in where I "came from" that when it turned out that the past looked different from what I'd imagined, a crisis of identity resulted. Who am I now that I've rewritten my family's history?

Not everyone lives this way, so tethered to the past. What would a life untethered look like, I wonder, a life in which the only place I am from is the place I happen to be? Would it be a better way to live? Less painful? Is it even possible to make such a choice?

The laminated map of Newtown is back in its place up on the wall, though it's now creased and worn from guiding me through ghost-filled streets. As I study it, compelled as I am to do so each day, I can't shake the feeling that none of this—the travels, the bitter discoveries—has happened by chance. What sort of cruel joke is the universe playing when it turns you into an expert (via researching and writing one dissertation, a translation, and a book) on Lithuanian complicity in the Holocaust, only to reveal that you, yourself, are descended from one of the complicit? What is this journey if not a spiritual challenge or ethical quest? What does it mean that instead of bridging the gap to the past, I've now broken from it? Has the quest, I wonder, been a success or failure?

Long after coming across the misshelved notebook at the Kent State University Archives, and after translating and digesting hefty passages from it, I located Ona's original interview tapes in a dusty archive in Chicago. Over the preceding decade, digital technology had caught up with me, and references to materials whose traces had once existed only in card catalogs now appeared in Internet searches. This time I was hardly surprised. When I found a reference to cassette recordings of Ona's conversations about Siberia, I calmly called the archive and arranged for copies to be made in time for my upcoming trip to the city. A friend drove me to the South Side to collect the five compact discs.

For weeks, I put off listening to the interview. The idea of hearing Ona's voice unsettled me. I needed time and privacy to face her, to go back to 1977 when everyone was still alive. So I decided to bring the recordings on a solo road trip.

After pulling out of a gas station, I slipped the first disc into the player and braced myself for the sound of Ona's voice. It sounded higher in pitch than I remembered, and I noted again what a sharp, funny, and talented storyteller she was. Still, there were few surprises in the recordings, since I had read and reread the Kent State transcription. Because of the letter (signed by a certain Kazys) that had introduced the interview, describing it as "a bit of a mess," I kept expecting the sound quality to deteriorate dramatically. But this never happened. With the exception of one or two glitches, I could easily understand what Ona said.

As I listened to that voice, both familiar and strange, I began to wonder if all those ellipses and fragments that filled the Kent State transcription said more about the transcriber than the text. What I had previously read as unraveling now seemed tightly bound, and what I had earlier interpreted as impending senility now resembled garden-variety absent-mindedness. No doddering old lady, in late October and early November 1977, Ona was sharp, quick witted, and verbose. I loved this version of her.

In addition to several hours of the recorded interview (this, despite the letter's description of the discussion as rushed), the discs included the taping of a dinner party with Father Joseph's relatives. Unlike the self-consciously performed interview, the conversation at the table was spontaneous and natural. I heard a group of people eating, their compliments on the food, and the clinking of glasses and silverware. The first voice, Ona's, broke in midsentence, telling a story about her friend, the priest. She imitated his voice, laughing, and then added how fortunate she and the other exiles had felt to have such a man in their midst.

The priest's relatives pressed her for details: How had he viewed collectivization? Had he been openly critical of the regime?

"I couldn't really say," answered Ona, not answering at all. She added that Father Joseph had always predicted that communism would be temporary, that the era would pass, and that the Germans would lose the war.

Finally the conversation turned to her experience.

"When I arrived in Canada," she said, "I found grandchildren who were bigger than my kids when I left them."

"And when you reunited with your children, did you not find that there was a rift between you?" asked a male voice.

"Of course! I felt that these weren't my kids. These weren't my grandchildren."

"Were there painful occasions? When you felt that they couldn't understand you?" the male voice pressed her.

"Well, they were somehow very foreign to me. The customs are very different here, so I had to adjust. You need to adapt. And the overabundance here, the material excess . . . I had to adjust a little bit." She said this matter-of-factly.

"I imagine it was a bit sad for you at times."

"Yes," she answered more quietly this time, "a little bit." Then she added with more certainty, "But you have to adjust." Back to her normal volume and clip, Ona stretched out her vowels: "We had to be happy that we were all together. Now, all of us were together. All of us were here."

After a pause, she changed the subject and told how Father Joseph used to eat a little charcoal from the fire, washing its bitterness down with water when there was no food. To the outrage and revulsion expressed by her dinner companions, she responded lightly, "Well, now, they say charcoal is good for the gut."

The words echoed through me as I drove. My grandmother's voice washed over me, and suddenly I too tasted the ash in my mouth.

Notes

CHAPTER 2

5 **"we tell ourselves stories"**: Didion, *White Album,* 11.

CHAPTER 3

7 **Its name translates as Newtown**: Today the city is called Kudirkos Naumiestis.

9 **"There is enough space for anyone"**: Goldberg, map of Naishtot (Newtown).

10 **"My intention in making this map"**: Goldberg, map of Naishtot (Newtown).

CHAPTER 4

11 **The words "Lithuanian Soviet Socialist Republic's Secret Police Committee (KGB)"**: Šukys, KGB search file.

CHAPTER 6

19 **In 1937 and 1938 the Great Terror**: Cohen, *Victims Return,* 2.

21 **Police reports from that era**: "Iš Klaipėdos siuntinėja 'ZYGĮ.'"

21 **What's more, the regime change**: Balkelis and Davoliūtė, *Maps of Memory,* 15.

25 **Over six successive nights**: Snyder, *Bloodlands,* 190.

25 **Despite a widespread belief**: Davoliūtė, "Kultūros istorikė"; and Anušauskas, *Teroras ir nusikaltimai žmoniškumui,* 8, 235. Davoliūtė cites 3,000 (8–9 percent) Jewish deportees. In its conclusion to Anušauskas's volume, the International Commission for the Evaluation of the Crimes of the Nazi and Soviet Occupation Regimes in Lithuania cites 2,045 Jewish deportees from Lithuania. Anušauskas estimates that 12.5 percent of the exiles of June 1941 were Jews, 72 percent were ethnic Lithuanians, 11.4 percent were ethnic Poles. Russians were also among the deportees from Lithuania in June 1941.

25 **Historians have now discovered**: Anušauskas, *Teroras ir nusikaltimai žmoniškumui*, 32.

CHAPTER 7

27 **They told her the state would confiscate the rest**: Geisler, "Gendered Plight of Terror," 110.

27 **The Gulags, meanwhile, were largely male**: Mason, "Women in the Gulag"; and Applebaum, *Gulag*, 287.

28 **Dated June 14, 1941, the statement reads**: Šukienė, Soviet Ministry of the Interior file.

28 **Ona's files from the Soviet Ministry of the Interior**: Šukienė, Soviet Ministry of the Interior file.

31 **"How does one survive"**: Galeano, *Book of Embraces*, 243.

CHAPTER 8

33 **A number of survivors**: See Oshry, *Annihilation of Lithuanian Jewry*.

33 **According to historian Saulius Sužiedėlis**: Sužiedėlis, "The Burden."

CHAPTER 9

36 **Patrick Desbois, a French priest**: Desbois, *Holocaust by Bullets*.

36 **"to kill all Jews as such"**: Snyder, *Bloodlands*, 188–89.

36 **In video testimony gathered in the 1990s**: See the oral history interviews of Ona Bečelienė and Julija Steponavičienė.

36 **Once everyone was dead**: See the oral history interviews of Ona Bečelienė and Julija Steponavičienė.

36 **Anthony's KGB file is vague**: Šukys, KGB search file.

37 **Locals refer to what took place next**: Vilna Gaon State Jewish Museum, *Holocaust Atlas of Lithuania*. It states that the date is unknown, although Isaac Glick (Izaokas Glikas), who appears later in this chapter, placed it on July 4.

37 **Most of what we know about these killings**: Glick recorded a detailed interview. See Glikas, Shoah Foundation interview.

38 **In all, 192 men were killed**: Vilna Gaon State Jewish Museum, *Holocaust Atlas of Lithuania*.

CHAPTER 10

39 **G—— was the son of Newtown's pharmacist**: Isaac Glick told me the surname of the pharmacist and his son. Romas Treideris, who appears later in this text, confirmed it. I believed their accounts then and have since found G——'s name and surname on a list of accused shooters archived in an obscure corner of the Internet: "Murderers of the Jews." Nonetheless, in the absence of a trial or official charges, I have chosen to refer to him and others like him by their initials only. In part I do so

in deference to the descendants of the pharmacist and his son, in the knowledge of how painful such discoveries about ancestors inevitably are. I do, however, name those who were tried and convicted because their identities are a matter of public record.

40 **A man named Vyšniauskas claims:** "Kudirkos Naumiesčio žydų žudynės Žynių kaime," Vilna Gaon State Jewish Museum, *Holocaust Atlas of Lithuania.*

CHAPTER 12

45 **There were, of course, some Lithuanian rescuers:** I have written at length about the rescuer Ona Šimaitė in *Epistolophilia.*

45 **the prewar Lithuanian Jewish population numbered 160,000:** This figure does not include the region of Vilnius that was not part of Lithuanian territory during the interwar period. By 1939, after the Vilnius region became Lithuanian territory, the country's Jewish population had grown to 250,000.

46 **In fact, the number of Jews killed by the Germans:** Snyder, *Bloodlands,* 342.

47 **Change happened so quickly:** Siekierski and Sousa, "Agents of History."

47 **Comprising more than 1.2 million files:** Siekierski and Sousa, "Agents of History."

49 **One purpose of such trials:** Prusin, "'Fascist Criminals to the Gallows!,'" 4.

49 **"They can be useful, sometimes critically important":** Saulius Sužiedėlis, personal communication, February 11, 2013, my emphasis.

49 **Lithuanian authorities tried to rectify this:** Kinzer, "Lithuania Will Evaluate Pardons."

CHAPTER 13

51 **Historian Arūnas Bubnys more recently put the number:** Bubnys, *Genocidas ir rezistencija;* and Vilna Gaon State Jewish Museum, *Holocaust Atlas of Lithuania.*

CHAPTER 14

56 **I know of two additional survivors of Newtown:** Isaac Glick told me these stories when we met on May 29, 2014, in Kaunas, Lithuania.

CHAPTER 15

62 **Members of these local forces:** Saulius Sužiedėlis, personal communication, February 11, 2013.

64 **The experimenter instructed the teacher:** Milgram, "Perils of Obedience."

64 **A sizable majority**: Milgram, *Obedience to Authority*, 33.

65 **"They refer not to the 'goodness'"**: Milgram, "Perils of Obedience."

65 **I believe that a great number of those Lithuanians**: I first started thinking about the notion of terrible obedience after reading Dieckmann and Sužiedėlis, *Persecution and Mass Murder of Lithuanian Jews*.

65 **"And why, if you please"**: Arendt, "Personal Responsibility," 31.

65 **"No one can force you to kill"**: Arendt, "Personal Responsibility," 18.

CHAPTER 16

68 **In 1944 before they shot him**: Romas Treideris told me this story when we met in May 2014.

CHAPTER 17

72 **"a mean old scene"**: Greenhalf, *It's a Mean Old Scene*, 25.

CHAPTER 18

80 **While sifting through one of the boxes**: The boxes contained the letters and diaries of the Holocaust rescuer Ona Šimaitė. Since I looked through them, those materials have been relocated to Vilnius University Library's Rare Books and Manuscript Department. My grandmother's interview remains archived at Kent State University. See Šukienė, "Kunigas Juozas Vailokaitis Sibire."

81 **"I do not think it is possible"**: Lawrence Ries, personal communication, May 21, 2015.

83 **"being visited by similarly uncanny moments"**: Weschler, *Everything That Rises*, 1.

83 **"Had Judd first got"**: Weschler, *Everything That Rises*, 31.

CHAPTER 20

87 **Rather than beheading**: Gentes, *Exile to Siberia*, 49.

88 **They offered to buy indigenous Siberian girls**: Gentes, *Exile, Murder and Madness in Siberia*, 174.

88 **Often these women marched**: Gentes, *Exile, Murder and Madness in Siberia*, 28.

88 **By 1941, the year the USSR**: Mukhina, *Germans of the Soviet Union*, 55.

88 **In contrast to my grandmother's seventeen years**: Šukienė, "Kunigas Juozas Vailokaitis Sibire."

89 **Some say he was repaying**: Terleckas, "Nauji mitai, išplaunantys ribą tarp gėrio ir blogio."

CHAPTER 21

91 **Some deportees speculated**: Purs, "Official and Individual Perceptions," 41.

91 **New arrivals huddled**: See Grinkevičiūtė, *Lietuviai prie Laptevos Jūros*.

CHAPTER 24

105 **Several months after I returned**: Kenna and Sayles, "The Distribution and History of Nuclear Weapons."

108 **By the end of 1941, two-thirds**: Sullivan, *Stalin's Daughter*, 126.

108 **"As many Soviet prisoners of war"**: Snyder, *Bloodlands*, 182, emphasis in the original.

108 **"The more of these prisoners die"**: Quoted in Dieckmann, Toleikis, and Zizas, *Karo belaisvių ir civilių gyventojų žudynės Lietuvoje*, 229.

108 **Captives were counted**: Snyder, *Bloodlands*, 176–77.

109 **Each week, the camp's commando**: Dieckmann, Toleikis, and Zizas, *Karo belaisvių ir civilių gyventojų žudynės Lietuvoje*, 242–43.

109 **"Panic-mongers and cowards"**: Sullivan, *Stalin's Daughter*, 136.

109 **"a dangerous, fainthearted, cowardly element"**: Order 270 quoted in Dieckmann, Toleikis, and Zizas, *Karo belaisvių ir civilių gyventojų žudynės Lietuvoje*, 221.

CHAPTER 25

111 **In the absence of men**: Mukhina, *Germans of the Soviet Union*, 119.

CHAPTER 26

115 **They prepared dishes**: Mukhina, *Germans of the Soviet Union*, 125.

115 **"Yesterday, it was grasses with grains"**: Šukienė, "Kunigas Juozas Vailokaitis Sibire."

115 **Millions of people**: Mukhina, *Germans of the Soviet Union*, 59.

115 **Category One workers**: Mukhina, *Germans of the Soviet Union*, 76.

116 **"Where are you supposed to find"**: Mukhina, *Germans of the Soviet Union*, 111.

117 **When my grandmother traveled**: My aunt, Ona's elder daughter, told me this story one day in 2009 over coffee in her kitchen.

CHAPTER 28

120 **The traces of this request**: Šukienė, Soviet Ministry of the Interior file.

CHAPTER 29

122 **"It is difficult for most people"**: Sullivan, *Stalin's Daughter*, 190.

122 **When the potato crop**: Mukhina, *Germans of the Soviet Union*, 58.

123 **He called it the "Urals method."**: Khrushchev, "The Secret Speech," 84n.

123 **With one last glance**: Alliluyeva, *Letters to a Friend*, 18.

124 **A million people found themselves**: Dobson, "'Show the Bandit-Enemies,'" 22.

124 **Ultimately, between April 1953**: Dobson, "'Show the Bandit-Enemies,'" 34.

124 **Some grew so desperate**: Dobson, "'Show the Bandit-Enemies,'" 25.

124 **Fueled by the groundswell**: Davoliūtė, "We Are All Deportees," 109, 136.

124 **According to Ministry of the Interior documents**: Šukienė, Soviet Ministry of the Interior file.

CHAPTER 32

135 **"Since 1942 she has been working"**: Šukienė, Soviet Ministry of the Interior file.

CHAPTER 33

139 **She was one of eighty thousand people**: Balkelis, "Ethnicity and Identity," 70.

CHAPTER 35

144 **"I didn't know that he was such a good person"**: Šukienė, "Kunigas Juozas Vailokaitis Sibire."

CHAPTER 36

149 **"It was like coming home to family"**: Šukienė, "Kunigas Juozas Vailokaitis Sibire."

CHAPTER 38

155 **Other deportees saw**: Cohen, *Victims Return*, 71.

155 **"ranged from happy to tragic"**: Cohen, *Victims Return*, 71.

CHAPTER 40

159 **In the 1977 interview**: Šukienė, "Kunigas Juozas Vailokaitis Sibire."

CHAPTER 42

165 **"I couldn't really say"**: Šukienė, sound recording.

Bibliography

ARCHIVAL SOURCES

Bečelienė, Ona. Oral history interview. Parts I and II. RG-50.473*0014. April 17, 1998. U.S. Holocaust Memorial Museum. http://collections.ushmm .org/search/catalog/irn508568.

Glikas, Izaokas (Glick, Isaac). Shoah Foundation interview. 11411. March 10, 1996. U.S. Holocaust Memorial Museum.

Goldberg, Ralph. Map of Naishtot (Newtown). RG-26.002. U.S. Holocaust Memorial Museum.

"Iš Klaipėdos siuntinėja 'ŽYGĮ,'" Valstybės Saugumo Policijos Kauno Apygardos Dienynas Nr. 108. 1938. F378-13-69. Lithuanian Central State Archives, Vilnius.

Šimaitė, Ona. Diaries. F286-17. MSS. Vilnius University Library Rare Books and Manuscripts Department.

———. Personal Papers. F244. (Mikšys Collection) MSS. Vilnius University Library Rare Books and Manuscripts Department.

Steponavičienė, Julija. Oral history interview. RG-50.473*0132. December 15, 2005. U.S. Holocaust Memorial Museum. http://collections.ushmm .org/search/catalog/irn518730.

Šukienė, Ona. "Kunigas Juozas Vailokaitis Sibire." Transcript of interview with Vladas Butėnas. November 2–3, 1977. Kent State University Archives.

———. Letters, personal collection of the author. 1947–65.

———. Sound recording. Interview with Vladas Butėnas. Cassettes 1–5. November 2–3, 1977. Jonas Sakas-Sakevičius Fond, World Lithuanian Archives, Chicago.

———. Soviet Ministry of the Interior file. V5-1-33649-1. Lithuanian Special Archives, Vilnius.

Šukys, Antanas (Anthony). KGB search file. K-30-1-1479. Lithuanian Special Archives, Vilnius.

Vailokaitis, Juozas (Father Joseph). KGB file. K-30-1-1815. Lithuanian Special Archives, Vilnius.

PUBLISHED SOURCES

Alliluyeva, Svetlana. *Twenty Letters to a Friend*. Translated by Priscilla Johnson. London: Hutchinson, 1967.

Anušauskas, Arvydas. *Teroras ir nusikaltimai žmoniškumui: Pirmoji sovietinė okupacija, 1940–1941* [Terror and crimes against humanity: The first Soviet occupation, 1940–1941]. Vilnius: Margi raštai, 2006.

Applebaum, Anne. *Gulag: A History*. New York: Random House, 2003.

Arendt, Hannah. *Eichmann in Jerusalem: A Report on the Banality of Evil*. New York: Viking Press, 1963.

———. "Personal Responsibility under Dictatorship." In *Responsibility and Judgment*, edited by Jerome Kohn, 17–48. New York: Schocken Books, 2003.

Auster, Paul. *The Art of Hunger: Essays, Prefaces, Interviews*. New York: Penguin, 1997.

———. *The Red Notebook*. New York: Penguin, 1997.

Balkelis, Tomas. "Ethnicity and Identity in the Memoirs of Lithuanian Children Deported to the Gulag." In Balkelis and Davoliūtė, *Maps of Memory*, 46–71.

Balkelis, Tomas, and Violeta Davoliūtė, eds. *Maps of Memory: Trauma, Identity, and Exile in Deportation Memoirs from the Baltic States*. Vilnius: Institute of Lithuanian Literature and Folklore, 2012.

Binkienė, Sofija. *Ir be ginklo kariai*. Vilnius: Mintis, 1967.

Bubnys, Arūnas. "Genocidas ir rezistencija: Holokaustas Lietuvos provincijoje 1941m.: Žydų žudynės Kauno apskrityje." *Lietuvos gyventojų genocido ir rezistencijos tyrimo centras* 2, no. 12 (2002): 81–99.

Cohen, Stephen F. *The Victims Return: Survivors of the Gulag after Stalin*. New York: I. B. Tauris, 2012.

Davoliūtė, Violeta. "Kultūrinė istorikė V. Davoliūtė: Tremtys buvo sulietuvintos ir 'sukatalikintos.'" Manoteises.lt, April 5, 2016.

———. "'We Are All Deportees': The Trauma of Displacement and the Consolidation of National Identity during the Popular Movement in Lithuania." In Balkelis and Davoliūtė, *Maps of Memory*, 107–36.

Desbois, Patrick. *The Holocaust by Bullets: A Priest's Journey to Uncover the Truth behind the Murder of 1.5 Million Jews*. Translated by Catherine Spencer. New York: Palgrave Macmillan, 2008.

Didion, Joan. *The White Album*. New York: Simon & Schuster, 1979.

Dieckmann, Christoph, and Saulius Sužiedėlis. *Lietuvos žydų persekiojimas ir masinės žudynės 1941 m. vasarą ir rudenį: Šaltiniai ir analizė*. The Crimes of the Totalitarian Regimes in Lithuania 3. Vilnius: Margi raštai, 2006. Translated by Rasa Adomaitienė, Paulius Ališauskas, Juras Barauskas, Ray Brandon, Jūratė Dvarionaitė, Rasa Sakalaitė, and Rima Zamuškevičienė as *The Persecution and Mass Murder of Lithuanian Jews during Summer and Fall of 1941: Sources and Analyses*. Vilnius: Margi raštai, 2006.

Dieckmann, Christoph, Vytautas Toleikis, and Rimantas Zizas. *Karo belaisvių ir civilių gyventojų žudynės Lietuvoje, 1941–1944*. The Crimes of the Totalitarian Regimes in Lithuania 2. Vilnius: Margi raštai, 2005. Translated by Rasa Adomaitienė, Paulius Ališauskas, Juras Barauskas, Ray Brandon, Jūratė Dvarionaitė, Rasa Sakalaitė, and Rima Zamuškevičienė as *Murders of Prisoners of War and of Civilian Populations of Lithuania, 1941–1944*. Vilnius: Margi raštai, 2005.

Dobson, Miriam. "'Show the Bandit-Enemies No Mercy!': Amnesty, Criminality, and Public Response in 1953." In *The Dilemmas of De-Stalinization: Negotiating Cultural and Social Change in the Khrushchev Era*, edited by Polly Jones, 21–40. BASEES/Routledge Series on Russian and East European Studies 23. New York: Routledge, 2006.

Erslavaitė, G., et al. *Masinės žudynės Lietuvoje, 1941–1944*. Vol. 2. Vilnius: Mintis, 1965.

Galeano, Eduardo. *The Book of Embraces*. Translated by Cedric Belfrage with Mark Schafer. New York: Norton, 1991.

Geisler, Irene Elksnis. "The Gendered Plight of Terror: Annexation and Exile in Latvia, 1940–1950." PhD diss., Western Michigan University, 2011.

Gentes, Andrew A. *Exile, Murder and Madness in Siberia, 1823–61*. Basingstoke, Hampshire: Palgrave Macmillan, 2010.

————. *Exile to Siberia, 1590–1822*. Basingstoke, Hampshire: Palgrave Macmillan, 2008.

Greenhalf, Jim. *It's a Mean Old Scene: A History of Modern Bradford from 1974*. Bradford, UK: Redbeck Press, 2003.

Grinkevičiūtė, Dalia. *Lietuviai prie Laptevos Jūros: Atsiminimai, miniaturos, laiškai*. Vilnius: Lietuvos Rašytojų Sąjungos Leidykla, 1997.

Kenna, T. C., and F. L. Sayles. "The Distribution and History of Nuclear Weapons Related Contamination in Sediments from the Ob River, Siberia as Determined by Isotopic Ratios of Plutonium and Neptunium." *Journal of Environmental Radioactivity* 60, no. 1/2 (2002): 105–37.

Khrushchev, Nikolai Sergeyevich. "The Secret Speech." Special Report to the Twentieth Congress of the Communist Party of the Soviet Union. (Closed session, February 24–25, 1956.) Translation adapted by Jon Bone. http://novaonline.nvcc.edu/eli/evans/HIS242/Documents/Speech.pdf.

Kinzer, Stephen. "Lithuania Will Evaluate Pardons in Nazi Collaboration Cases." *New York Times*, December 25, 1992. http://www.nytimes.com/1992/12/25/world/lithuania-will-evaluate-pardons-in-nazi-collaboration-cases.html?pagewanted=all.

Kruk, Herman. *The Last Days of the Jerusalem of Lithuania: Chronicles from the Vilna Ghetto and the Camps, 1939–1944*. Edited by Benjamin Harshav. Translated by Barbara Harshav. New Haven: YIVO Institute for Jewish Research, 2002.

Mason, Emma. "Women in the Gulag in the 1930s." In *Women in the Stalin Era*, edited by Melanie Illič, 131–50. London: Palgrave, 2001.

Milgram, Stanley. *Obedience to Authority: An Experimental View*. New York: Harper & Row, 1974.

⸻. "The Perils of Obedience." *Harper's Magazine* 247 (December 1973).

Mukhina, Irina. *The Germans of the Soviet Union*. BASEES/Routledge Series on Russian and East European Studies 32. New York: Routledge, 2007.

"Murderers of the Jews of Rokiskis, Sakiai, Seirijai" [*sic*]. https://docs.google.com/document/d/1qJsEVXef2C_TMMoUsQ2P7QlcFYku A8smrgGuB5_sP4I/preview?pref=2&pli=1.

Oshry, Ephraim. *The Annihilation of Lithuanian Jewry*. Translated by Y. Leiman. New York: Judaica Press, 1995.

Prusin, Alexander Victor. "'Fascist Criminals to the Gallows!': The Holocaust and Soviet War Crimes Trials, December 1945–February 1946." *Holocaust and Genocide Studies* 7, no. 1 (Spring 2003): 1–30.

Purs, Aldis. "Official and Individual Perceptions: Squaring the History of the Soviet Deportations with the Circle of Testimony in Latvia." In Balkelis and Davoliūtė, *Maps of Memory*, 29–45.

Siekierski, Maciej, and Richard Sousa. "Agents of History." *Hoover Digest* 14 (January 2010). www.hoover.org/research/agents-history.

Sinclair, Upton. *The Jungle*. Cambridge MA: R. Bentley, 1971 [1906].

Snyder, Timothy. *Bloodlands: Europe between Hitler and Stalin*. New York: Basic Books, 2010.

Šukys, Antanas. *Du mediniai ir trys geležiniai kryžiai: Atsiminimai iš Lietuvos nepriklausomybės kovų, 1919–1921 metais*. London: Nida, 1964.

Šukys, Julija. *Epistolophilia: Writing the Life of Ona Šimaitė*. Lincoln: University of Nebraska Press, 2012.

Sullivan, Rosemary. *Stalin's Daughter: The Extraordinary and Tumultuous Life of Svetlana Alliluyeva*. Toronto: HarperCollins, 2015.

Sužiedėlis, Saulius. "The Burden of 1941." *Lituanus* 47, no. 4 (2001). http://www.lituanus.org/2001/01_4_04.htm.

Terleckas, Vladas. "Nauji mitai, išplaunantys ribą tarp gėrio ir blogio, arba nesaikingai nupudruotas J. Paleckis." *Kultūros barai*, November 16, 2011. www.delfi.lt/news/ringas/lit/vterleckas-nauji-mitai-isplaunantys-riba-tarp -gerio-ir-blogio-arba-nesaikingai-nupudruotas-jpaleckis.d?id=51633721.

Tory, Avraham. *Surviving the Holocaust: The Kovno Ghetto Diary*. Edited by Martin Gilbert. Translated by Jerzy Michalowicz. Cambridge MA: Harvard University Press, 1990.

Vilna Gaon State Jewish Museum. *The Holocaust Atlas of Lithuania*. http://www.holocaustatlas.lt.

Weschler, Lawrence. *Everything That Rises: A Book of Convergences*. San Francisco: McSweeney's Books, 2006.

⸻. "The Judd Ant." In *Uncanny Valley: Adventures in the Narrative*, 29–31. Berkeley CA: Counterpoint, 2011.